Phantom Kangaroo

AN EERIE PLACE FOR POEMS

For the poets and artists
and interdimensional beings

ISSUES

NOTE FROM EDITOR

November 2010
(Inaugural issue)

Witnessing something paranormal and finding a new favorite poem are one and the same. Often times it can't be translated, or no one believes me, so I just sit and brew with wonderment. For a moment, I'll be enlightened to some secret of the universe and all the cells in my body will align with planets and stars, and I will understand myself wholly and completely, as a human being and as other things I could be. And then it fades. And I continue to be bits of neurosis, of habits, of fears, and all I felt for that short time no longer influences my choices.

I was tired of this happening, so I wanted to gather poems of paranormal qualities all in one place, for proof that these things exist. Hopefully it will awaken something in you, and you will believe that you are meant to be in this moment, reading these poems, and it'll confirm your existence, and when you tell someone that you caught a glimpse of your purpose, hopefully, they'll believe you.

May 2021

This book was a decade in the making. Or maybe it always existed. In these pages you will find 300 poems published in Phantom Kangaroo over the course of ten years — issues 1 through 23.

Phantom Kangaroo remains a portal to everything that is shrouded in mystery. It can be dark at times, but it is never bad. It is questions and glimpses and testimony. It is real and a hoax and theories. But in its earthly form, it is poetry and art and beauty.

If while you are reading this, you get a strong sense that you belong here, visit phantomkangaroo.com for how to submit.

Claudia Dawson
Founding Publisher & Editor
Phantom Kangaroo
claudia@phantomkangaroo.com

They watch from the running gaps between stars

the planets are protons

I, in death, become a wave of thought.

— "Scopers"
Alex Brown, page 4

ISSUE NO. 1

"a tempest"
ron koppelberger

Revenge of the pumpkins
Bill Gainer

It rolled from the porch
and laid there like a rotting corpse.
Flies and gnats
flew from its mouth,
it turned soft,
took on an odd odor.
The dog rolled in it
and was banished from the house
until after
the first big rain.
The lawn died
where it fell.
Two full seasons later
and still
nothing grows there.

Scopers
Alex Brown

They watch from within the walls

whisper secrets in frequencies a human ear cannot decipher

their station formed, the mad ones have tuned in.

He breathed into their bones and twisted eardrums about

signals freshly intercepted, feeding them what to do

in the term informing about the zoo.

They watch from the running gaps between stars

the planets are protons

I, in death, become a wave of thought.

Since the children
David McLean

since the children have been loving absences
and things not moving, working seven to eleven
at murdering themselves more or less
competently, more or less because
there is no such thing as infantile,
or any other kind of, sexuality

predefined; since then there has been a slow rolling blues
playing inside them like spiders on acid with heroin
eyes, though they might not know what the blues is
though they might never have listened to it,
since the children have been living
suicide in slow motion,

the skull in them has been singing,
but no body will ever listen —
after all, they are just children,
new things are always living

Sleeping with demons
Laura LeHew

I see the queen in her cups—
eight swords restricted
by a wolf moon.

I see Lust's first blush
flesh on flesh on flesh
thrumming to be unbound.

I see the queen stand unbridled
a westerly wind
in opposition.

I see an innocent woman,
a man, a boy, from Tulsa,
destroyed.

The hanged man in anger.

The death.

I see the danger.

Satanic Relics
William Doreski

An appendix to my Field Guide
to Evil offers instructions
for devising Satanic relics.

The bones of an infant's arm
upholstered with dried seaweed
and boxed in carefully carpentered

hickory or ash, for instance.
One is not encouraged to murder
a child but find one killed by bombing

or other act of war, then purchase
the sad little corpse from parents
whose grief seems authentic but

subject to the flux of currency.
Another example needs stones
washed down the River Jordan

all the way to the Dead Sea. Fill
a skull with these stones so tightly
it doesn't rattle; seal the eyes

and neck-hole; cement the jaw shut;
then gild the assemblage and pose it
on your mantle where dinner guests

will find it charming. Still another
requires the ashes of a blood
relative dead of natural causes.

Mix the ashes with clay and throw
a pot on a hand-cranked wheel;
glaze and bake; use the pot to store

pebbles from Mecca, Medina,
Nazareth and Jerusalem.
Of course such relics can't function

in our nuclear world; but I hope
that hearing about them relieves you
of otherwise obtuse gloom.

My hands were cold the day I learned how to tell time.
Laura Hardy

The guests were tall like church pews. Devouring stale crackers, giving their
bad breathed goodbyes. The iridescent pearls at my mother's collarbone bit
at my flesh. I studied the splintering prayer bench far from my dangling feet.
The Autumn air had stolen the moisture from our skin. Cracks in my fingers
became salted cracks in the concrete. My eyes traced them to the water's
edge. Gold and blackened leaves waltzed over the plastic blue cover. Below
the surface a shadow of the dead rippled my skin. Fear itself whimpered
explicitly from the balding trees that grains of sand were pounding at the
bottom of my own hourglass. I ran back inside as wind chimes played their
funeral march.

On a clear night you can see for never
Harry Calhoun

Light being what it is, immutable, and we know
how long it takes us to notice anything
changing, and we should know how long
it usually takes for anything to change.

So we should be amazed to see
something that no longer exists?
We're not talking dinosaurs here,
or ghosts, or gasoline at nineteen point nine

a gallon. Look up at that canopy
the pine trees in your back yard hold up tonight
and see Lord knows how many stars
gone nova and not really there

any more. And others whose demise
is light years in the future, like an aneurysm
bubbling somewhere in your brain,
cozy as comfort but a universe away.

Keep looking at all those stars
as if they are all still here
not fading slowly into

something else

The farsighted bandit
Melanie Browne

When it came
to love,
he was
a prowler,

a nocturnal
smuggler,

he hunted
her in the
darkness,
swooping down
mid-air,

you could hear
her screeching
through the
thin walls,

in the mornings
he walked her
to the train station,

one hand on
the back of her
neck,
the other
stretching
out his talons

The teeth of wraiths
Felipe Rivera

Dedicated to the unknown, the absent, the untouchables,
Huddling, nurturing, crooning over simple shadows
A lingering scent of groping lust
Deaf parrots in cosmic solitude dressing and disrobing
And breaking cadavers in infinite jazz:
A severe gash outside our bodies
Scribbling with cut tongues, or fates
Tracing the tip of each delicate hair
A field of naked poppies, days before the solstice
A sperm-tinctured blanket mist and Mount Sutro
Indeterminate like time, or now, or dusk
Breaking wine glasses, screaming into black holes, or rum
Lips torn into existence

We are night or shade
Beautiful blind monsters smashing mirrors in reverse
Always absent and untouchable
Like two moons passing with no word
Now stuck to flesh made raw
On this furiously gentrified corridor
Where sighs sigh the shape of a jail cell
Of lavender, musk, or the Pacific

Have you been crushed, crumbled, returned to the earth
Medieval Madonnas levitating
Coated in rust where there is no rust
Always absent, unreachable like free wine, or infinite jazz
Lingering in scent, groping lust
Inside the folds of an old eye, a bruised dress
Our terrible duty is to see it to the end

Huddled and crooning over a simple light
To the singing children, the ill-fed and the well-fed heading for the abyss
To the unknown, the phantasms, a shadow or mirror, to the moments of silence
This is our dedication:

For an unborn child
Michael Grover

Last night a psychic touched me
Rested her head on my chest
Looked up at my surprise & said
Oh your ex had a miscarriage
That was the story that she gave me

I saw you only once in a dream
You were riding in the backseat
Beautiful bi-racial girl
Beautiful curly hair
Beautiful smile
Your mother in the passenger seat
I driving
It was a smooth riding luxury car
We were all happy
Life don't work out that way

Your name was to be Karenthia
From Jean Toomer's "Kane"
The most beautiful girl in town
The one the boys all chased around

Today you would have been eight
Going on nine
We would probably be living
In the ghetto of West Philadelphia
We would worry about you
Walking the streets every day

You died before you ever
Had a chance to live
She told me she had a miscarriage
It was really an abortion
She had to erase
Every trace of me

Today I place flowers on your grave
Somewhere in my head

Today I send this Poem like a prayer
That you were born in a better place
And you are living a happy healthy life
Things would not have been good here
I doubt that life would ever be as smooth
As it was in that dream

Last night a psychic touched me
As she rest her head on my chest
She reminded me of you
It's been years since I've thought of you
No wondering where you would have
gone to school
If you would have been a decent person
I cried

Hallowe'en
Maggie Armstrong

Happiness was never the intent of our lives. We had only wanted to smoke cigarettes, one after another after another, and not cringe at our self-mutilation. When I'd open our fresh pack of whatever was on special I always imagined my face cracked and puss filled, like I had already been burning in hell for a lifetime or three. Then when I'd put the fresh cigarette in between my rouged lips my face would go back to normal. No burns, just pink. I always felt like Freddy Krueger sitting next to you.

Arachnophobia was on the television set with a Jack-O-Lantern on top. Flickering in unison with each scream. I looked down at my puke green nail polish against the grape couch. The middle nail still black from the hammer incident two days before. I started having nightmares about you. We'd wander around an abandoned mall like in Dawn of the Dead only nobody was after us. We'd just hold hands and walk, excited about which store to loot first. Nordstrom? We could raid the Marc Jacobs collection. Cinnabon? No calories in the post-apocalyptic world. The high ceilings of the mall were draped in darkness. No electricity. We could barely see the signs outside the stores. And when we'd get there, there were no cinnamon buns fresh from the oven. Only boxes of weird ingredients with labels in Swedish or Aramaic. No Marc Jacobs sweaters, only poly-blend tube tops with bedazzled diamonds on the seams. I finally squeezed your hand in horror only to receive a fist full of bleeding spiders. You were never there.

Lollipops, Tootsie pops, Almond Joys, and Dots. Your favorites. We'd only ever buy your favorites, and in bulk. At this time of year, when I close my eyes to smell the nutmeg and burning leaves, I always picture that day at the Nut tree. Our first pumpkin patch fair. I only see hay, big blocks of hay in the back and foreground and then someone hands me a pumpkin ice cream cone. I look down and see the tiny brown flecks in the flesh colored mound. I imagine the flecks are your freckles and the ice cream is your face. I bite down hard and let the cream drip down from both corners of my mouth. I look to mom, hoping to see her scream at my sister's blood dripping from my mouth. She doesn't see me when I stand next to you. You and your beautiful freckles as you suck on a bright red tootsie pop.

Lost you again. You crawled under the bathroom stall and locked it from the inside. You slid the hammer under the stall and told me to swing. If I got a thumb we'd try and find the toy store. You said you saw flashlights back in the abandoned Starbucks. You said the wick wasn't strong enough. You said I should never let the candle go out, not even when we got the flashlight back. If we got separated we should meet at the Spirit Store. It was the easiest to find in the dark, the only store with electricity. You could hear Michael Myers' groans from anywhere in the mall.

Opera is my favorite horror movie because it is your favorite horror movie. My favorite part is when the killer tapes those knives to her victim's eyelids so they can never shut them. You told me Dario Argento wrote it that way in order to suggest that we all crave an audience. Even psychopathic killers need validation. You handed me a knife once, out of boredom I suppose, and you told me to cut you. Just for fun. When I took it from you the blade was cold, but the handle was still warm. You told me everybody ought to have a few lacerations and scars, so we can tell the boys in bars something other than what retail outlets and strip malls we worked in. When you asked me to cut you, your gaze skewed slightly above my head. I turned around to see, and there was no one there. Only the oven door with your reflection in the window.

Werewolves of London by Warren Zevon blast out of the speakers behind me. Again. Whoever was throwing this party took the time to freeze little severed heads in ice and put one in each cocktail. I snuck off to the bathroom to add more of my own vodka from my pink flask to the blood red cocktail. I didn't feel like sharing. I sipped the new mixture and turned the lights off. I've started chewing on my cheeks again. Slowly biting off bits of my own flesh and swallowing. The cranberry vodka stings the wounds, but I take a big gulp and swish it around to amplify it. The glow from my digital watch illuminates my face a tender green, scattering shadows across my face and hollows out my cheekbones. I take another sip and spit it all over the mirror.

The amorphous blobs migrate down and over my eyes. I think to call on Bloody Mary. Bloody you, Mary. Would you recognize me now? Would you recognize me through my metamorphosis, into the Halloween version of me? The full moon version of me? The worst version of me?

Eleven thirty five AM is when they found you. You were completely naked except for your angel wings. The police never could figure out why they only took you. Both of us were standing on that street corner, admiring the scratching and howls of the fall foliage blowing across the blacktop, but they only wanted you. With your beautiful pumpkin freckles.

Eleven hours after you were taken is when they found you. I slept in my Frankenstein costume, weary of taking off the last thing you saw me in. You died remembering me as a green monster with bolts sticking out of my neck. I would always be a green monster in your eyes. You always made me feel green. Eleven Halloweens are all we ever had.

Nausea is all I feel now. Festering in me. I want to eat eleven times a day, to fill the void you left, only to vomit up and on my shoes so I can eat again. You left me with a scar I can talk about to strangers and strange men, but with no wound to heal. When I think of you in the oven's reflection I am at ease. As much as I miss the smell of your skin and the way your hand felt in mine, I am grateful for your absence. I miss you more than words can share, but I love you better dead.

Swirl
Howie Good

Your tongue,
a swirling storm,
finds me,

and, Bingo!
the Ukrainian church
shouts,

flowers pop
heart pills,

the fish can't
sleep because
of the noise,

the leaves
so green
they're almost
black.

Bridesmaid, radiology
Taylor Graham

Fluorescent corridors, ghost-
girl in hospital gown,
braces on legs and ankles. Pale eyes
as if she got here
falling down stairs till there was nothing
left of bones.

You're worried about your ankle,

and here's a girl so sadly
beautiful, she begs for rhyme. Seizures,
she says. Like falling from a high-
rise helispot. She'll miss
her best friend's wedding. Seized
like trying for flight.
Bones too brittle-thin,
lovely as a bird shot down.

They'll x-ray your ankle.

We'll walk out in late spring
daylight, drive familiar streets,
the freeway, country roads haunted
by a ghost, back home.

"bleed"
leila a. fortier

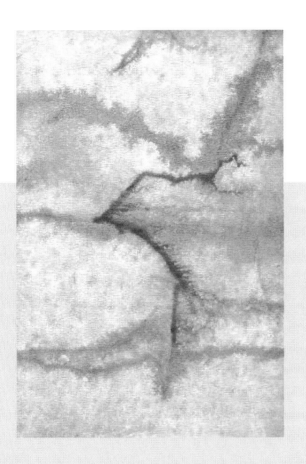

ISSUE NO. 2

*Even in our sleep we emit radio signals.
There'll be no patience for evolutionary chaos
down the line. We must imagine the things
we cannot see. Emeralds, lemons, and blood
everywhere. We all have our own secrets to
keep.*

— "A quiet evening in the debriefing shed"
Jane Røken, page 20

The monster says:
Ruby Darling

*You piece of shit, you worthless
whore.*

but you were prepubescent,
gravity hadn't swallowed your youth,
you still thought about things
like why grown-ups are lonely,
why they fight,
why they do bad things to children,
or why they do bad things,

then your brain got consumed with
perfection
and pleasing, and you wanted to
please,
like most people do
who don't know what they stand for,

and there was the monster
seeping under your skin,
when it was pale,
the way Macedonia ticks do from
Greece,
or maybe just Northern California
ticks do,
since thats all
you really know,

his venom spreads,
corroding your sense of self,
and you
detach,

*You piece of shit, you worthless
whore.*

Soon your sunken eyes avoid mirrors,
and all the disgust and dead

and deceit are purged from your
veins,

you run,
and you keep running until you feel
euphoria > deceit > purity
and you forget the salty of sweat,
how nice to hold his hand,
the awkward wet of his palm,
but you didn't let go,
didn't ever want to let go

instead you starve,
starve and believe you are no longer

the memory is buried in your liver,
but you stay focused on self-loathing,
no more wasteful obsessions,
like :-) or ;-) ?
or the melodrama of laughing out
loud,
so instead you think about things
that aren't waste,
like why lovers give up their power,

and then, maybe you give in,

your brittle heartbeat > slower more,
you taste death,
the dryness of your mouth,
the persimmon you once ate before it
was ripe,

IVs are stabbing your unwed veins,
and it's nice to feel something,
and your body is barely,
and your mind is barely—

maybe this is what hail feels like
against a windshield,
and it would be nice to snowboard

again,
without it breaking your bones,
but maybe breaking your bones would
feel nice too,

and you sink into your mother's last
words:
you look like an alien,
and you take it as a compliment,
and the monster pats you on the back,
he owns you now,

76 pounds of your flesh
left for him to eat.

Death of a love poem
P.A.Levy

by autumn it was flat lining
red passion cells all pale and iambic
come winter it was stone cold dead
natural causes
its heart just stopped beating

we said prayers
with lowercase tears in our eyes
they rhymed as they rolled
down our cheeks
until they mingled with snivelling snot
then it became a mucus mess

now i'm haunted by a ghost-writer
a white page with two full stop eyes
giving it the scream of space
like the empty bed
or the room without you
trace smell of perfume
and all the words that were never said

Silent, we-
David Tomaloff

underneath the city,
on top of the moon,
bruises ring the new
year's song; a hymnal []

a battle plan : mace
and mesa" eloquent
trees above sway to
songs of inebriated

;   soil-
mix,   locate, enounce,
change speed,   and playback-

chance lift, and bullet(!) to the
music
-we a/drift to"

9how silent is   :us
and   how silent
[en dash]   the moon.

Ed Gein
Mike Meraz

some of the sanest places
are the cities
take away the lights and cameras
the hustle and bustle
of the big town and all you have are
loneliness, fields and farmlands
the perfect place for murder.

Father, again peering
Donal Mahoney

The final years dear Mother she
was never, well, what actors call "on
location."
Physically, of course, we found her

everywhere:
the parlor reading,
the kitchen ironing,

the basement sweeping,
unlike Father whom we never found
though he was always there.

On Sundays when he went to Mass,
he'd stay behind, peering.
Like Queeg, he'd stare

from under or behind
whatever he wasn't
hiding in front of.

Lathe sick
Lawrence Gladeview

insomniac machinist
ninety pounds insubstantial
bodysnatcher zeal—
vertebral loner

soot tissue lung
ketonic exhalations
you deserve
a kool cigarette

washer gasket slip
sanguine hemorrhage
prune five to three
right dominant now left
dependent

florid foreman fuck
scar shelled belly
duct tape triage
company dime bottom line

maimed machinist
diner ashtray life
knife out tongue
dearest cherry pie
promptly acidulated.

The worm
Jim Bronyaur

It starts from within
the darkest thoughts
reality never felt so good

The space of time
not endless
the chime is the heartbeat
hours come and go like breaths

It moves
It twists
It shifts

A calling from feet away
miles, maybe years

You hear a rattling
a wet noise
thinner than blood
but deadly

Not at once
but within time
never an ever lasting moment
time eats it
can you feel it?
spinning in motionless heaven
pushing where it shouldn't
a bulging you see

The world feels
the pressure
time holds like a vice

A moonlit walk
only reveals
how lonely we all are
how consumed we can become

how the worm can turn its head and
bite
what does it look like to you
do you know its there
eating you
becoming you
taking all your time
all our time

Embrace not erase
the picture yells
give more than take
in your mind
silence
there is no blessing here
just the worm

Push. Nibble. Turn. Bite.

Tarot reading, 1/8/03
Janann Dawkins

The land of milk and honey is all about you.
These rivers of food are angels
whose bodies have broken in their fall,
broken into bounty. Their disembodied wings
curve into shade trees, orchards shoring the bank.

You fear scorpions in your path, but in truth
the path is a woman, mild and white
like light. You are walking up her breasts.
Your feet are bare and true. Your toes
sink into her tresses.

I. Five of Staves
II. The Emperor
III. Four of Swords
IV. Eight of Cups
V. Three of Cups
VI. Temperance
VII. Queen of Cups
VIII. Page of Swords
IX. Three of Staves
X. King of Staves

The last alien abduction
Michael Frissore

(Based on an Otto & George Joke)

They pulled me in like Al Pacino
in the bad Godfather movie, and
I felt the light and the heat engulf
me like a nuclear holocaust.

And then there was nothing,
unconsciousness or a stoppage
of time, but it was all blank.
I woke up and, sure, my ass
hurt, but we all expect that now.

A bunch of them pushed me off their
spacecraft like a houseguest who had
long overstayed his welcome, but I
grabbed a pen and a comment card
on the way out, both with the aliens'
address and phone number on them.

And I knew I had them.
This time I had them.

Ghostly ka-nunnah
Richard Peake

was an animal science fiction writers
might copy when seeking a nightmare beast
to create chills in movie goers
whose desire for scary films knows no bounds.

Do striped tiger ghosts stalk Van Diemen's Land?
Do zebra wolves haunt Tasman nightmares?
Captive thylacines died in foreign hands.
Too late, ka-nunnah received protection.

Tasmanian tigers got a bum rap.
Thylacinus gynocephalus lurked
in Tasman outback to offer mishap
to the ranchers' sheep that proved too tasty.
True, thylacines liked sheep, but took the blame
for feral dogs and wily bushrangers.
Called striped wolves, these predators' native game
was kangaroos and wombats, not fat sheep.

It was a hunter, killer of mammals
whose sixteen dark vertical stripes revealed
wolf-like, ferocious beast chimerical.
Bounties on their heads, thylacines died out.

Or did they? They lurk in man's memory.
Almost every year people claim they've seen
marsupial tiger shadows pass slyly,
ka-nunnahs sneaking through outback brush.

A quiet evening in the debriefing shed
Jane Røken

Listen. I'm going to explain everything. They come in threes, like Souzhong tea, sloe gin, and belladonna. We've been subject to a slip of reason. They walk among us already. The malediction bureau is not to be trusted, the distant early warning tapeworms are no longer under our control, and a fair number of surveillance subs have transmogrified into turnip lanterns. Just because we cannot see them, it doesn't mean they're not there. And we've had reports of inexplicable disappearances: riverboats that sail off into nothingness, travellers who vanish while crossing a field. What you see depends on what you think you're seeing. Take for instance the ballroom upstairs. It's the kind of place where things go out of hand after midnight. This is going to be a filthy job, at odds with the drip and drone of humanity, demoralized until the crack of doom. Even in our sleep we emit radio signals. There'll be no patience for evolutionary chaos down the line. We must imagine the things we cannot see. Emeralds, lemons, and blood everywhere. We all have our own secrets to keep.

The Chariot (The Victor)
Nic Alea

roma

i.

i'd tattoo, solar plexus,
onto your chest.
tagging your skin
to the vibration
of needle pin
pricks,
like
bombing the side of a subway car
and i'd crawl inside you
like a gothic tower
and you'd still be branded.
and i'd tattoo
amethyst
onto your rib cage

and the cursive letters
would dig into your
bone
and you'd rub dirty
fingertips
along the grooves.

ii.

you'd think of crystals
and how you'd clean them
with moonlight
after you kissed the base of my throat,
scraped my skin with calcite,
i'd suck on
tourmaline
for healing,
'til it drained

all salt from my body,
and you'd use my skin
to stretch canvas'
and paint water color landscapes
onto my stomach
and suns on my chest
and moons into my labia
with silver paint,
it fades against
human flesh,
but when stretched
it turns parched,
and i'd settle for
a ply wood cross.
dress me in white linen
stained with pomegranate seeds
that you found in meadows
of poland
and i could sing you
into a sound from between
my phantom wings,
are you tired, roma?
from wandering
like
fingertips moving along
prayer beads,
shouting hail mary's
into the starving sea,
tell me, roma,
can i make you sacred
like your prayer shawl
of silk weave?

iii.

in a wedding dress
you fell backwards
started speaking in tongues
that were cut into the sky
branded hieroglyphics
and you thought to birth children,

but instead
let me flip tarot cards onto the base of
your throat,
then let me sculpt you into a
consecrated icon,
and when you plucked iris petals with
your mouth,
i saw your eyes,
my god,
i cried.

iv.

sometimes i ask you
if i can count the tree rings round
your eyelids,
count your age in nature,
tap into your turquoise politics
of the river
and then i told you,
in what words,
i do not know,
but the truth,
the soil is where you
would stretch your limbs,
roma,
when they come to hear you fight
with body movements
they will wrap their wrists in rose stems
and hope that you settle
into solid ground
enough so your legs become
ivy and your feet stretch roots
into the earth's chest cavity
and you sit still
at the edge of the river's sanctuary
and you whisper like a scorpion
an ancient prayer hymn
and the moon takes your
song
and reveals herself to you.

and one more,
queen of swords (the crystallizer)
holy wood

i burn paolo santo
because the shamans call it holy
wood
and i call myself brother
like they do on mountain tops
where orange draped spirits
carve hiero into tree trunks,
do you want me to make you holy?
would you carry raw ocho gemstones
in your pockets
if you knew it meant
you could eat
without feeling guilty?

i tried purging on words that
sacrificed demons
and i played fiddle to some magnolias
tied ribbons round these taste buds
and i wonder
how the monks
in the angkor region of asia
felt about food,
i wonder if they kept diaries
counting calories
or skipped meals
as if the hollowness of their
stomachs wasn't to feel closer
to a higher power
but to feel as
thin as the bones
that structure them

and i come from California
and i come from a place where
womyn think skinny is a compliment
and front lawns are littered with silicon
and you can't find your front door step

without tripping over
the fault line of superficial beauty
and i say
that my parents raised me right
to think outside the boundaries
of the pressure peers put on me
but that's not to say
that when mainstream media
and classmates told me
that a size 16 was ugly
i couldn't help
but remove myself completely
let tally mark scratches
on my hip bones become distracting
so i could forget lines on
bathroom scales
and focus my time looking
for the one thing
to gag me
and spit up day old adderall
to reverse words like "you fucking
fatty".
and I still refer to food
as the biggest demon
to ever slay me
but those trials are slowly sinking
beneath me
and i see progress on the daily
of womyn creating goddesses
out of their bodies
as it should be

i still call myself brother
like the shaved head spirits
peering over mountain tops
just observing
the delicate efforts we put
into self destructing
and i still pick at my food
with wooden spoons
that i carved out of

paolo santo
and i burn it
because the smoke rings mean clarity
and my gut isn't
so much sunken
and it brings me back to
that place in california
where i'm from and i can
envision
a forest made of real bodies
and i can envision never again speaking
the words, "they hate me because
of what they see"
and i've learned that beauty
can be manifested
by power of believing
that skin deep
is so far from the reality
of me

so i'll burn paolo santo,
so i'll burn holy wood
for you
if you'd like to see me
and i'll tell you
some stories
about trees
and fallen leaves
and we'll eat
the letters and consonants
off the plate
and yeah we'll
eat
and yeah we'll drink
and yeah we'll finally be merry.

Asleep
Jason Brightwell

The room was bathed in flowers
sobbing down stink and staining walls.
There you lay, sleeping. But void of that
innocent dreamlike smile.

Carelessly, you left candles burning.
I blew them harshly, hoping to wake you.
But you lay there, oblivious to
my trespass and interference.

Your constant slumber infuriated me.
I remember moving to strike you
and hitting a crucifix.
You weren't asleep at all.

Afterwards, returning home to remove
Suits and masks, I met mother in
the kitchen. Angry that she lied.

"earth { +ling"
david tomaloff

Sometimes I feel so close
to death that I dream I am rubbing
the bones of my father's spine

poking out of his back.

– **"Since my father died"**
Harry Calhoun, page 33

Francesca, I had an affair
Nathan Logan

You will haunt me when you die.
I know because you say, "Nathan,
I'm going to haunt you when I die."
Whoa-whoa-whoa-whoa.
First, we need to attend a party
with a piano player and coat check.
I need to tell our guests that you think
a bed sheet is not a good fashion choice
for walking around the neighborhood.
I need to write a little poem about it—one
where you do ghost stuff in a ghost raincoat.
I'll call it, "Francesca, I Had An Affair,"
and the audience will believe I am awful.
They'll wait for your disembodied voice.
They'll want to ask about your raincoat.

Star-bellows on the train blow their horns
Shannon Elizabeth Hardwick

Star-bellows on the train blow their horns.
I am happy, one exclaims,
for my mother was a sage-tree and my father, a thorn.
I ask them for a naming, a way to move through pain.
Oh simple, another says,
your body's a shell you'll break out when you're ready,
with your own horn to blow and miles, yes mountains worth
of snow to burrow the forgetting, to graciously love everything
turned to ash and bone

Euripides
Roxanne Broda-Blake

The bright ring of atomies
crowns the actor,
stepping through a cold time river
in the throes of a scream.

Suicide in a palace
Tanuj Solanki

A dozen testimonies
of the queen's fetish for doormen,
stand outside the palace facing east,
facing the rising sun
that smiles with a blessing on their lives.
Remnants of last night's drizzle darken
the colors of the palace sandstone,
reddened yet awaiting further reddening,
as yellow light strives to enter royalty.
The thirteenth doorman sleeps inside,
for the first and the last time,
in a room that has seen
regicide, patricide, and fratricide;
his hand is over the queen's dark hair—
a status quo from last night.
Knowledge of the fetish evades him,
as the secrets reside in the queen's bosom.

The dozen is puzzled in their own minds
'Oh, the ways of the regal esoteric.'
But the erotic memory of royal treatment,
makes them look over their shoulders
in comic curiosity
to decipher from hints the happenings
of the latest night in the oldest room.
The queen wakes up first,
and advances to the balcony,
in a robe that tells the dozen

'Oh, the physical has transpired.'
Little clouds of jealousy surround them,
as dark clouds of rain surround the palace,
swiftly,
instantaneously.

The queen ponders the events
of a night where she loved,
loved with passion,
and promise and hope,
and a beckoning of eternity,
crushed by a perfection
she thought couldn't exist.
A single tear drops down her left cheek,
and somehow manages to sparkle
in the cloudy morning of the now grim day.

The dozen watches with intent
the changing hues of the queen's countenance.
And though each of them is lustful,
each of them depraved,
their jealousy mixes with happiness—
the weird happiness that emanates
from knowing the one you might have loved,
is loved.

And then in the next instant,
the queen jumps from the balcony;
head hitting the sandstone floor
of the courtyard,
blood gushing in a random flow
on the flatness.
Death comes swiftly, even before
the dozen arrives to look for it.

The thirteenth sleeps smugly,
and the room witnesses suicide.

Cyan graveyard
Scryer Veratos

Cajun spice arises the fallen
The obsidian casted solstice is upon us.

"yes we are Indigo, we are Glitter Fog London,
basking in the uranium caskets that held us."

Bombs leave amaretto salts that evaporate skin.
Hope is put into the entrancical dance between natives.

"so sumerian smiles will alude us, the azure anunaki as gold cats
find our tombs, they cry. We should not be revived."

Majesties ill usions render the messiah's power useless.
Unless mephtaphysical rare knowledge becomes
a unified vision.

"And grey pellucid tears move synnically down my Icarus cheeks.
I flew too fervently, and your verbosity didnt quite match your malcontent."

The ultimatum,
magenta and cyan must converge atop the promised lands
highest point.
Deceased synergy must be used.

"We are the platinum eyesight,
the vicariuos splitting maul
and you will never unknow us."

Sunny's too tavern
Cynthia Linville

She dripped red across four time zones –
nail polish, hair dye, ink, blood –
trying to stay ahead of the refrain
that chased her like a flood.

In Barstow a honky tonk shaman –
fingers trembling on guitar strings—
called her to the altar
at the motel across the street.

She touched him as if he could heal her
his thigh-vein pulsing her fingers
slightly off-tempo
to the music in her ears.

In the morning they felt like two skeletons –
teeth on teeth when they kissed –
and she drove on towards Mexico
still listening for the music she missed.

Discovered
Joseph M. Gant

there was time, now past
when discovery was
of all things new
and unmolested by experience.
but now as the scene of some crime
itself, discovery
lays beaten, waiting in dark corners
with panties tied around its ankles,
gagged and begging guilt from hapless grins.

Limbo
Peter Schwartz

h.
staying alive takes two hands
but the implied traffic of having slept in a bed
weighs shadows by an open
window

f.
reflection's not the only light that matters
so I've sold myself to a future version of myself
hoping someday my feet might
taste the ground

s.
your shoulder's a church
I can't forgo, an igloo of salvation
melting in the tropical heat
of your defenses

l.
which marathon taught your legs
to cry when the pavement soured
from the very natural losses that
come after so many miles

e.
space is a kind of god, stretching
out forests already named after the fires
that will destroy them, elbowing
out the darkness

c.
cardiac secrets wobble in my chest
like bowling pins, thunderstruck
registering only from the neck up
as I massage the day away

k.
soft sacrifice, my knees have hardened

into olive pits, the temperature of the earth
when it's saddening in place
the removal of bird life

w.
the circumference of my shame
amplifies itself like music nobody wants
to hear, buried waist-deep in mud
I hear everything

Broken at the waist
Felipe Rivera

Where Nature and Sanity blur or consciousness,
A buzz and static, noise, and warmth
A perversion, pervasiveness of virility and dog shit
Crisp, clear, unobstructed,
From outside, inside like a zombie, headless
Chicken (in communion with the corpses)
A three is an orange, but more like a red
Thunderous monotony, a wild horse
Instinct and words that hide others, the true ones
Like an insect shedding with a heavy body
Clumsy, grinding, finding letters, sent and received and never sent
Not agile but just a single unit
Impaled with sloth
A single white pillow, smeared, heavy with makeup
And oil and stale, faint smells of resting
Heads of unwashed hair, faces
And muffled cries of (you fill in the blank)
That hair brushing her cheek, her brow,
Her jaw, her chin
Her eyelashes fluttering before
Nightfall

Astronomical rabbit
Jennifer Phillips

<pre>
      Born   late
        to the   cross
            in   Ares
          pale wood
          rabbit bucks
          fate to know
        why sunlight only
      hides the darkness
        why   firelight
      of bile   burns out
        all matches and
        why   moonlight
      runs across   wet faces.
</pre>

The Anger Tree
Luis Cuauhtemoc Berriozabal

God has planted the seed
of anger in my mind.
How could I stop feeling
angry, if God created
these feelings inside me?

I pray to Buddha too.
When I bet on games
I tell Buddha I will
stop believing in him
if I don't win.

The anger inside me
grows like a tree.
It is God's tree, with
apples and snakes,
and I am no gardener.

I cannot prune the tree.
I cannot cut the anger.
It is God's doing and
I don't want to go
against God's creation.

Since my father died
Harry Calhoun

Sometimes I feel so close
to death that I dream I am rubbing
the bones of my father's spine

poking out of his back.

But those are isolated instances.

Most of the time
I feel as if I'm riding a train
woefully behind schedule,

its whistle trailing ghostlike
Into the constant night behind me
clattering slowly but surely

over the low and gentle hills
of his living backbone.

To beckon a perfect lover
Laura LeHew

1.
know that it is time
rip up your wish list
be gone illustrious white knights—
unredeemable damaged beyond
repair types
unlock the possibility

2.
cop an attitude
dress to your best asset
add a touch of leather
remove one article of clothing
go unfurled into the world

3.
invade his personal space
hold eye contact
whisper a question
touch your would-be lover on his
shoulder
fold him into you

ISSUE NO. 4

*Fear darkened my heart
so I kneeled on my teeth
gone away to rejoicing her.*

— **"Hibiscus tea "**
John Swain, page 36

"con-trails"
jennifer l. tomaloff

note: jennifer
l. tomaloff's
photograph is
the inspiration
for ed
makowski's
poem featured
in this issue.

Dave's con-trails
Ed Makowski

Working in a basement
computer warehouse
with one other man
who was hired
before me, so
          naturally
he had seniority

and played
conspiracy theory radio

We worked between
40 and 60 hours per week
listening to radio shows about
time travel, chupacabras,
grays (slang for aliens),
poisonous con-trails,
the bloodline of Christ,
werewolves and vampires,
unidentified flying objects,
abnormalities in weather
and
everything was caused by
government experiments.

A dusty decades old
basement with poor lighting
on land that had been
Native American marsh.
Deforested, drained, filled.
Then paved and built to become
new retail opportunities
in mid-century America.

When Dave started seeing men
walking about in loin cloths,
and vanishing, I wondered
what had taken them
so long.

Graveyard nights
John Grey

The only white he knows
is tombstones,
your neck,
another moonlit canvas
to mark with dates, with death,
for pointless flowers
to rhapsodize
as they wither
in the shadow
of your decay.
Even touch does not fool him,
the cemetery bed
pandering to
his dark expectations,
your life sucked out
through grave-digger lips,
as bitter cold marble
rises up into his fingers,
your flesh stiff and pale
as the bone
it clings to.

It's all in the wrists, said Ted Bundy
Donal Mahoney

The others, of course, are more rabid than I
but less apt to show it.

Whenever I strike, I never romp off.
I stand with the wrist that I've snatched

from the lady locked in my teeth
as I wait with a smile for the wagon.

As one of the few wrist-snatchers
still on the streets of Chicago,

I make all of my rounds in old tennies.
I dive for the purse hand, give it a whack,

and sever the wrist without slobber,
then stand like a Vatican Guard

with her wrist in my teeth until
I am certain I have no pursuers.

In my dreams every night I can see
all of those women whose wrists

I have had in my teeth.
They stand at their bus stops

like Statues of Liberty,
shrieking and waving their stumps like flares

as I wait for their screams
to bring to a freeze

the patrol cars glowing
in the middle of the street.

Hibiscus tea
John Swain

Field became another sky
when snow fell
over the first winter night.
In the drift on the hill
we warmed beneath my coat
and sipped hibiscus tea
from a silver bowl I carry.
Trees floated from the ice
as she polished a rabbit jaw
and dropped prayer beads
to mark our path.
Fear darkened my heart
so I kneeled on my teeth
gone away to rejoicing her.

Preserve the lies
Ben John Smith

Bach composes violoncello minute
and at thirty-eight seconds
she walks into my room
and cringes at the sight of me
pouring wine into a pint glass.

And her eyes break
like Christmas tree
decorations.

Or a plug that has
never been
unplugged.

She says,
"What in GOD'S name are
you doing?"

And with an ugly truth
I lower my head

like a child with dirty palms
and say,

"I'm pretending to be famous."

She whispers to God.
The cat brushes past her
bare
feet.

I don   t know what
she said

or if he heard

but I bet
he doesn   t
need her
as much
as I do.

Stockton, California
Anthony Jones

hearing train tracks rumble late at night
locomotives bellowing like wounded dogs
a fog gray feeling
seeming sometimes blue

The pornographer's daughter
Laura Hardy

Lets go to the moon and dig a giant hole.
So big in fact only our arms will penetrate the surface,
we will reach out just at the top,
our fingers will dance as blue flowers for our graves.
Then we will walk downstairs to Beirut
and laugh, as the men we have been inside stare,
trying to remember why our hands look familiar.
We will answer seductively, "Monsieur, do you not recall?
I performed your colonoscopy" and he will glare,
looking down to see his hands are sewn to dull gold cymbals.
We will drink as he serenades us,
Bang, Bang, Bang.
Then it will start to rain.
So we will pull down the roof and build a house of cards to stay warm.
One hand inside our coats and another up our skirts, because
lesbian porn is all that works
and we swore we'd never be wives but only sleep with their husbands.
Then we will hear a cry.
The pornographer's daughter, she stands tall in the mirror
unable to gaze upon her naked self.
Touch and feel are so very far apart.
We will climb her tower walls with suction cups made
with the chicken cutlets we left in our brassieres.
And take her down, down, down,
to the bridge, where guards shelter her shy cunt.
Even they will trade kisses for liberty,
and the pornographer's daughter will turn red in the cheeks,
I'll press my finger to her rouge, spread it on his lips whispering,
"Freedom Rings!"

Because out here we know that:
Bare feet tell the best stories,
Sand can often be unkind,
Heat determines how much you smoke,
Rain cannot tear down a house of cards,
And you, like me,
Fall asleep with one, two, three,
But prefer to wake up alone.

The end, twenty ten
Tannen Dell

"I couldn't help but want to die when I started living; the Irony of all good things."

In the beginning, I did not know this girl. We dated in a dusty corner mansion with a scene broken movie as she talked not to me, but a parallel, through some shining veil of existence and as I walked the path of doomed concrete and mist grass, a dog of fog trotted up into a pencil outline and then sky fur apparition.

After I saved the fourth twin little girl with bone skin and tombstone hair, the human form of Cerberus' mother greeted me with open fangs.

—A shower at 4:00 AM later...—

In the beginning I did not know this girl until the computer screen told me she died in a nightclub. I doubted the coincidence and my girlfriend who had not been to that dream, or to that house.

I was in a camera as it snapped in half and should've woken up, but in the end the girl was wrapped in pinion feathers and a cross.

I will live and
The haunting house
Will remain forever unspoken.

"In the beginning Shadow created the Heavens and the Earth."

Voodoo dream
Ron Koppelberger

Spun by ebony threads in a voodoo dream,
By perfumed Hyacinth blooms and burlap cloaks of
Scarecrow design, the pin and needle by
Garlic seed and horseradish flavor,
The breath of a witch and wicked measures of
Bat blood.

We are all haunted

Megan Kennedy

She wanted to die young.

Her theory was,
All the enlightened and spiritually
Significant people
Didn't need to live that long.
To her, it was a badge of honor
To leave this place early.

She had formulated this
From hours of reading:
Philosophy, religion, biographies
Crime statistics, metaphysics
And fiction of the loftiest kind.
She said, I believe I have it figured
out.
The Hindus had it right.
Your soul will keep coming here
Over and over
Until you're ready to rejoin
The universe at its highest
understandings.
Those who die young
Well, they didn't need to be here
Any longer.

All the kids beaten and murdered
By loved ones and strangers.
All the angelic teenagers
Killed in traffic accidents.
All the world-changers
Who barely had time to
Give us their message,
To show us the light,
These people were, somehow,
Finally finished.

Martin Luther King. Jesus Christ.

JFK. RFK. Abraham Lincoln.
Dimebag Darrell. Some prodigy
Drummer from a metal band
I'd never heard of.
Heath Ledger. Princess Di. Anne Frank.
Jimi Hendrix. Hank Williams. Mozart.
Bob Marley. Joan of Arc.

She had a list
Longer than my arm.

I would point out some
flaws in her theory:
Gandhi. Mother Teresa.
Pope John Paul II.
Newton. Einstein.
Galileo.

Her arguments were:
The scientists were smart,
Not enlightened.
Gandhi just stood up for a cause,
And so do a lot of stupid people.
And Mother Teresa, well,
According to her own letters,
She couldn't even feel God anymore.
But she kept helping the poor anyway.
Wonderful, yes, but disqualified
In this particular running.

She is the only person I know
Who could trivialize Mother
Teresa And actually make you stop
and think about it.

And so, this is why, she,
My best friend and my own personal
Piece of enlightenment
Wanted to die young.
Because it would mean she was
On the right track,

Not only for her own ascension,
But for the overall well-being
Of the universe
And mankind.

 I said, why don't you
 just kill yourself then?
 Guarantee it?

But suicides don't count, she said.
It has to be an accident, or a murder,
Or some natural cause.
You can't cheat your way
Into that great gig in the sky.

And so she waits, every day,
Wondering if today is it.
Reading her Aurelius and Dali Lama,
Nietzsche and the Bible,
Aquinas and the Satanic Bible,
Alchemy, occult, fundamentalist Islam.
She keeps learning, and searching,
And by now, she can debate brilliantly
With anyone of any religion,
Any belief.
Now she is a force to be reckoned
with.

 I tell her, why don't you teach?
 Write a book?
 Keep a record of all these ideas.
 Who knows what may come of them?

But she just smiles from under
Her ratty old blanket
In her favorite armchair.
Sometimes she will reply:
Maybe I will.
But with any luck,
I won't have it finished
Before I go.

At water's edge
Taylor Graham

the embryonic stage of a creature
I've never seen before, sleek and
limbless,
dark as if conceived in a blackout.

Beyond, oblivious square-dance
of water insects on the still surface.
August afternoon. Overhead,

a republic of jays in noisy caucus.

But this creature — as if cloaked,
about to shed a shadow-habit, burka
of disguise.

The sun is lowering
as if on some malignancy in water,
mutation of air.

Twilight of changes coming.

Lost dialog
Helen Vitoria

let's say that there was no Ghost—
let's say, all the small conversations
are with you
& somehow you carried them back to the

Ghost, outside, on the front walkway
near the magnolia, because that is where the
Ghost would be, waiting for me to open the door
& let him in.

"things we dreamt in the fire—
{ #radio static as a form of modern blues}"
david tomaloff

ISSUE NO. 5

this part:
*   we shout sins until they form postcards*
*   papercut our tongues, papercut*
your politics, papercut my wrist so you can
put your mouth on it, as if you charmed me, and you do
but not anymore,   I think.

— "Letter When is for Wednesday; or How To Count"
Elena Riley, page 48

Reproaches from the dead
Amit Parmessur

pouring some blood-like whiskey into my old battered glass,
trying somehow to reach new heights of spirituality
outside, through the weak and decaying window
I could see the sky coming out of golden stars
in the neglected and stinking garden I could find
bloody buds sprouting out of the flowers left
in the distant darkness I could make out a few
angel-like persons coming out of the dead soil
my adorable grandmother,
my drunkard of a grandfather
and my brave girl
I shook my head;
was I drunk before drinking?
grandmother was surely coming to tell me
that I forgot to clean and embellish her grave last week
grandfather would ask me why I had
neglected his wife just like he did when alive,
but nothing about himself
I emptied the crimson glass in my trembling mouth
my dead girl knew that I had betrayed
the promise of never loving someone else
all due to that new girl next door
who strangely resembled her
the reproachful dead folk approaching
and stopping at the rickety garden fence,
I closed my freezing eyes,
plugged the juicy bottle mouth into
my own glass-cold mouth
and turned the bottle upside-down

A ghost about town
Claire Joanne Huxham

In the airport I stopped all the clocks
nonchalantly
and made an old man cry.
I had to do it eventually. Live the dream.
They say a spectre's haunting Europe –
well, I can tell you it's not just one,
it's a whole circus troop of them.
All chains that rattle and screams at night.
We've always had a bad name back home.
Cursed sprite, that sort of thing.
The whole of Europe's a cliché; a haunted house
where religion and history stalk the halls
shaking their gory locks.
I don't miss it, the Old World
with its cruel superstitions, the garlic hanging
at the window. Here the dead don't
crowd the streets and there's hardly any litter.
Only once, a Comanche woman nursing
a burnt child at her bloody breast.
She slipped
around the corner of the cinema,
scalps fluttering behind her like confetti.
Here, I can be who I want to be,
a ghost about town — I can reinvent myself
like the Madonna.
O America.
I'm an open road, an empty sign,
I'm a blank cipher.
I scribble a few words on a postcard
back to the Old Country
but my pen leaves
no mark.

The stevedore
Catfish McDaris

Unloading your poems
from a ship of fog, your
melody floats through
the ruby lipped prostitute's

Dreams, her long silky
legs wrapped around
the moon, a rose

Between her teeth, a
mocking heart song

Insanity rips & wanes,
blood drips saxophones,
the wind blows away
the thunderbolts.

Seven stones
Kevin Heaton

Gather high on a hill

at the revealing

     center

      of all goodness

Native woodwind fluted songs

                  sing

         wispy songs to happy
feet;

dancing through restoration quest,

and Wopela: Thanksgiving.

Awaken seven stones
with igneous passion force

Come

sacred fire ember glow   spit
sparks

through smoky mystery source

Spirit thunder west wind

grant hollow pipes creation breath

Eagle prayer, sky spirit conveyor;

transport receiver pathway sight

     north ,south, east, west,

impart the good, sweet cherry blood

Charlie Manson
Kyle Hemmings

I once dated a girl named Charlie Manson. In the early days, we walked along glistening beaches, holding hands, or me, holding my tongue, too afraid to speak, to ruin what hadn't yet begun. Her eyes were all about swept away, swept away, that sideways longing. Overhead, a seagull's wings melted into the sun. We listened to the splash. It was the way my mother died. Charlie told me that birds such as the one that chose drop instead of flight are more common than we think.

Squinting at the sun, she said that when someone can't forgive you, then you become that person. It was the sun that couldn't forgive that seagull.

We spent weeks wasted on bubblegum or leaving footprints in the park after ten. We necked and felt each other's broken teeth. We listened to Black Flag and bought Petticon's ink drawings of victims. Then she admitted it. She had a collection of glass bottles in which she kept the voice of every lover who ever rejected her. She flung the bottles from rooftops or into the sea. It helped to clear her head, she said, to stay clean.

Come clean with me, she said, making her eyes small and dirty peep-hole glass.

Then it was my turn. I left and didn't return her voice messages. Alone, I awoke to the new morning, the sun in stitches. In the mirror, I was glass-eyed and cracked. I wouldn't speak for years.

Letter When is for Wednesday; or How To Count
Elena Riley

parts:

you would destroy each other
you both read Lacan before I did

ok here:

my purple teeth streets
on your patched shoulder
when you fall over the brick stoops of nw
             where we pretend to be afraid and important
drink as if not remembering will change the shape of things
gold fish in the green bottle & a paper crane in my skirt pocket
             if this goes sour
but I hate sweet things,
which is why I'd rather be
sideways alongside you

this part:
      we shout sins until they form postcards
      papercut our tongues, papercut
your politics, papercut my wrist so you can
put your mouth on it, as if you charmed me, and you do
but not anymore,   I think.

I don't ask this time, don't indulge your narcissism
as you say, "you remind me of me of me, you know me?"
      or "don't you know who I was before?"
             and
             "but shattering is my favorite," you say or
did I say—saying I remember—don't I? don't you remember?

part:

so when you start reading to me,
and I imagine my soft back,

empty,
perfect, w the sheet
just so,
obsess, the toothpaste
in the left corner of your mouth (don't you remember who I said I
was?)
to remember you were disappointing.

Octopus
Matt Ryan

The sailors wanted to see eight little hands pop out of the water, eight little
hands to inspire an extended version of This Little Piggy Went to the Market,
because the market was where you could get milk for your honey. These
hands, legend said, induced ecstasy. Afterwards, they'd sing about going
home to their lover, who was waiting, not necessarily for them, not necessarily
this time, with hands open hoping for a treat, and hearts slightly ajar, encased
inside a container made of glass that anyone could see or break and
preserved with a saline solution. There was just so much salt in the air, the men
could feel it spelunking their taste buds. Salt was another gift they wanted to
give, not receive. The men at sea were well aware that octopus semen out
of context is disgusting. That's not what they wanted from the octopus. That's
not the sorta love they were looking for. Meanwhile, the men cruised around
praying, This'll do. Whatever is out there, is out there, but please be out there,
Octopus. Truth be known, these men might not find it. The octopus has so little
control of its arms and doesn't hear well, though no one speaks of this inside
the market.

Morning talk show, gentrified.
Matthew Specht

i dream in black and white, you know

i dream of trying to run in waist-deep water

i dream of punching enemies with all my strength but nothing happens

i dream of wet hidden warm places surrounded by soft skin and gratitude

i dream of the end of the world

(i have a bag of chips, my wits, and a towel

armed thusly, my dear, we are safe!!!)

i dream of newspapers as wallpaper yellowed from the effort it took

to tell me the president is dead

and the drive-thru lady knows i'm on the floor of the front seat

and the woods are NOT lovely, dark OR deep

they are rotten

and wet

and would not burn even if you doused them in gasoline

lit a match

tossed it in

walked away and

waited for the warmth

and when i dream the dream where i fall from great heights

i wake up

wondering

if i survived

*Previously published in bending light into verse, volume I.

Eternal recurrence of the same
Howie Good

He wouldn't take off his hat. To live well, he said, you must live unseen.
He had a rope around his neck and one leg already over the railing. A
passerby happened to notice the bank clock said 11:11. The most mysterious
thing is a fact clearly stated. I inquired at the desk. The sun will shine for
another six billion years. At least.

Knitting a ghost-thing:
R.D. Kimball

she opens her eyes and discovers a
room

plain cold jellyfish entrails
plasma phantasms which whisper
white whisperings

she stiffens her skin
at the touch of phantom limbs:
for she is due to make things
from the dead

doors open from every corner of her
mind—
the room an infinite polygon

stretches one side and another
and over and over
walls folded in on themselves

doors open from every corner
and welcome the beastials

she opens her eyes when they touch
her
and everything is violet,
they beckon her to follow them
into the many formless rooms
from which they spawn their
spawnings—

they call her a weaver

colors close their wombs around her
and in her sirensong the fading fades
across the pallor of her lips her skin

her eyes her hands

there is nothing but the ghostly thing
she knits
and gasping exhale violet mist:
she laughs her laugh in the between—
place.

she opens her eyes and discovers a
room
the infinite room
with the infinite beasts

and her outer world fades...
becoming a rumorghoul.
becoming an unviolet.

At the edge of a séance
Robert McDonald

This is the time when I think of your hands.

The scissored path of a swallow, skimming over a field of summer grasses.

Bette Davis, raspy and elegant, aching to light up one final cigarette.

Your fingers skittish as an only child, your fingers as wise as turtles on a log.

The threatened rain falls, violent, bountiful, not at all like the touch of your hands.

I am in love with the grandmothers who are ghosts in your hands.

A gypsy palm reader's erotic novel, written in the lines of your hands.

A grandmother drowsy, dozing on the sofa with the television on.

The cook's sweet cream sauce a ghost on your fingers.

Like crows flapping in a thunderstorm sky, like crones, like typists, like leaves caught on fences.

Remember a night they were twined in yours: my fingers little monks cloistered in your hands.

Come forth like Lazarus, move like swans.

Valentino manifesting with a turn of the wrist.

Think of a ship filled with all the heroes.

"Night" is a hauntingly beautiful installation.

Tell me anything: tap it in code on the kitchen table.

Marilyn and Joe
Melanie Browne

sitting in the
Archeus café,
the bombshell
movie star and
the Yankee Clipper,
and Marilyn leans
in and whispers,
"I think we're dead,
but isn't it lovely?"
and Joe looks
around the empty
joint, sunlight
dancing playfully
across empty tables,
says, "yes"
and squeezes her
hand a little tighter,
smiles a little wider,
tells a joke to get her
to laugh

Underspace
Walter Conley

one time i was sad
and another time
so, so sad
i couldn't tell the difference
between any—
or another thing

i thought of waking
then thought better
didn't have the strength to dream
stars glued to the ceiling
glowed
and shrank and
pulled away from me

after i lost sight of them
i tumbled through a
trap-door floor
where you were
and your eyes
your mouth
o, even your cold heart
were melting

something told me
then
to ask
if you could show me
the way out
but something else
—i'm guessing you—
said
"leave him alone"

"full of shadows"
megan kennedy

ISSUE NO. 6

Neither of us brave
enough to climb skyward,
to banshee our longings
loud above the grim
bottomless gash.

— "Under the yoke of inauspicious stars"
Nancy Flynn, page 61

PTSD
Donal Mahoney

In the waiting room, I squeeze
this old rosary a nun gave me
the day I got back from Iraq.

I was still in a daze on a gurney
and I still had sand in my hair.
Some of it remains, no matter

how many showers I take.
Sand from Iraq lingers, I'm told,
until you go bald, and then

you are able to concentrate
on other things.
What might they be, I wonder.

But today, in this waiting room,
I squeeze the rosary tighter
when I hear, louder than

the gunshots crackling in my dreams,
the real screams of that little boy
right over there, the one who's

rapped his elbow off the radiator.
Lord, listen to him scream!
Each week he comes with his mother

for her follow-up appointment.
He sounds like the jet
that takes me back at night

to that little village in Iraq
where the sand puffs up
in mushroom clouds

above the bullets
as the children scream

in their hovels louder

than that little boy
screaming over there.
Maybe everyone

in this waiting room
listening to him scream
can come with me now

to that village in Iraq.
Sitting here, I know
that boy's pain so well

that in my fist
this rosary no longer
knows my prayers.

Demi
Joshua Otto

Everywhere she strolls
lifting ancient tides

Seemingly to wait
only to disembark beyond
the least logical terminals

She approximates unlikely
ends with a shelled unwillingness of
method repeated as death claims

To be a matter of shifting papers
consciousness become infinitely small

Paralyzed by her deafening sleep
a stillness originally meant nothing

Before fire was
the mad text of space

Called her to care and be
sacred for us

After death
Khalym Kari Burke-Thomas

her torso is a rookery
of marmosets   one boys
another   after another
    boys another

boy

The memory of light
Jay Coral

Lucy snapped a self portrait
on the bathroom mirror
some said her irises were too slow
to react to the blinding flash
she was wide-eyed
to the ovoid clock
that melted at 3:00 a.m.
the white walls behind her
were warped like rippling waves
and the shake of the camera
produced an oblique double
some said it looked like her mother.

Shhhhh...
Joan McNerney

there is a
witch living
on the corner
where the four
roads meet.
Her eye is
evil, her
nose crooked.

She lays down
the tarot
pattern
with wrinkled
hands.

Asks "do you wish
tea of wormwood
or henbane?"

She will enchant
your mind now
into fields of
wild roses.

Dear student, because you are dead,
Nathan Lipps

there is an empty table that no one
will set. The time and place
is up to you. You are the mended
center piece. The 7.95 for a book
in its prime. You were
the words scratched above urinals.
You, dear, are the smell
of candles snuffed, of curtains
torn by huffing winds.
I sin everyday
to your name. I dance
in my towel, almost naked.
Clean water falling from my body
to the bare floor. Every drip,
every heel kick, is a nod
towards your granular scars
and red blooded taste.

Wane
Emily O'Neill

The boy with the broken wrist sits
at the lake's edge trying to curl
his fingers into a fist. The fingers won't
make it past the plaster. He'd like to know
he could still defend himself.

The girl with the phases of the moon
tattooed on her chest lets the ends of her hair trail
across the tops of her knees and says, "Baby."
Nothing else. Just, "Baby."
The boy stops moving.

He can see an entire month of sky strung
along her collarbone; in the dark
it looks like the crescent press of fingernails into palm,
so he places his palm on the space between her breasts,
reaches fingers for the weeks above them. She stares
at his thumb hooked under the curve of her
like a scythe. The plaster
cast makes her itch.

He reaches for blood.
Her heart murmurs.
He feels the hiccup, calls it
a ripple in the sky. If the boy could break
anything beautiful, it would be this moment.

The moon is not out this night. The lake
takes its place, a large silvery silence
they can toe the rim of,
fall through, drown in.

Phrenology
Lisa McCool-Grime

From the phrenologist, I have learned
to know myself as a country
knows its fences and rivers.
See the chart colored
like a map: the fissures, the swell
of organ tissue underneath
my scalp. These little hills
at the corner of my eyes
hold all the numbers
I have been thus far.
I am thirty and full
(feel the dormant volcano
at the base of my skull)
of wanting for someone to bless me
with touch. When I called
on the doctor, it was all metal
to sternum, plastic
to pulse and me
under the paper sheet
like a fruit fly under plate glass.
What good are his stirrups
for my heels? I should find my head
in the skilled hands
of a geographer, a man
who knows how basins came
to lie among the ridges of my crown.
When I call on the phrenologist,
he stands behind me as I sit,
nestles my occipital bone
to his navel and runs
a ringless ring finger
along my cheek, a sign
of peace across my brow.

Under the yoke of inauspicious stars

Nancy Flynn

You burn me,
a bundle of duty,
a pietà limp,
acute angle
in your arms.
We blaze
through Orion,
beyond Virgo
one more night
by the strip mine,
our backs a trail
along the strut
of the empty
water tank—
69 painted white
on its towering rust.
That's what
goes on here.
But not now, not us.
The valley below alit,
a nameless constellation
of lights, daytime's ugly
gussied up.
We hold hands,
your voice a precious
rumble, pea coal raked
as you speak
of saints and hate
and those who would
shut us off from God.
Our innocence held taut,
flamboyant in itself.
Neither of us brave
enough to climb skyward,
to banshee our longings
loud above the grim
bottomless gash.

El chupacabra
William Page

It's never taken alive, though in life they
say it leaves a scent of putrid death.
The triangular bite it's said to leave
on the breast of prey priests say
blasphemes the Holy Trinity. Without
fur or hair, its skin is smooth and usually gray
except for white amphibian scales rising
along its spine. Like ghosts it has no eyelids.
The eyes it's written burn with fire, though
others swear they're really moving silver mirrors.
At its rear is a thick python's tail. Its mouth
is fish-shaped but with long fangs and spiked
teeth that tear blood-sucked victims to shreds.
According to some accounts of those who've
heard of those who claim they've seen it,
the monster's forelegs are thin and shaped
like a small child's arms, and at its wrists
are baby's hands with claws. From
its dog-like snout long gray hairs grow,
and wreaths of smoke ensue say some
from its tiny but flared red nostrils.
The skin upon its hidden belly is black, but its
back and sides are gray, almost blue as bruises.
All who claim to have been so fearless
as to slay the night stalking creature swear
its black tongue is marked with red crosses.
It's been reported by Boy Scouts,
sworn to tell the truth, they've heard
in thick brush its squeals like a butchered pig's.
Its ears are long and sharply pointed said
a lady whose cat she cried was eviscerated
while she watched horrified from her kitchen window.
She testified it left a smell of sulfur when it fled.
Even if the Chupacabra's shot or poisoned
farmers tell it doesn't cease twitching its limbs
until all the blood it's sucked from goats and sheep,
and sometimes from deer or calves wandered from
their mothers lowing in the dark, puddles from its mouth

wide into a small pond. We must keep our children safe
inside and look for fearsome tracks, its rear feet like
a large dog's, its front a child's hands with claws.

Autumn cannibalism
Neil Ellman

(after the painting by Salvador Dalí, 1936)

When there is nothing left to eat
But your own conscience
(A delicacy of a kind)
Etiquette requires
That the women choose first
That the proper utensils be used
Spoon fork and carving knife
A napkin on the lap
To ensure civility.

It is a simple repast:
A stew of half-eaten body parts
A mélange of squabbles and feuds
Centuries old
(Too ancient to remember why)
Coming to this November meal.

"The thigh is best," says one,
"Especially rare
Full of flavor and revenge."

It is best in the autumn
When we feast
On the remains of dignity.

Red within
Steve Toase

When Red Riding Hood felt the leaves of the wood brush
against the inside of her ribs
she was confused and not a little frightened.
She was not the devourer. Her teeth were neither big or sharp, but small and
pearl like.
Yet still from deep within
she felt the breeze stir the branches of large, ancient pines.

When Red Riding Hood felt the footsteps
walk deep inside her a chill spread through marrow and nerve alike.
Another was the consumer. Her appetite was small and human
flesh not to her taste.
Yet she recognised the shuffling footsteps of one who told dark tales of her own,
with Red Riding Hood cocooned on her knee.

When Red Riding Hood heard the howl echo inside her
she felt faint and took to her bed,
then a smile crossed her face.
Maybe victory was hers, the tearer of flesh torn asunder himself.
Yet she felt needle pointed teeth bite and feast from within.

When Red Riding Hood saw the sparks from the axe sharpened
against her heart,
she closed her eyes to the starbursts of iron.
She didn't feel engorged,
her skin neither strained nor stretched
Yet she could feel the
chop,
chop,
chop,
as the cuts winnowed her away.

When Red Riding Hood tasted the woodsmoke and scorched fur on her tongue
she cried tears of pure glass
The words caressed her throat and ate the breath
until they flowed out of her mouth.
"Once upon a time, there was a little darling damsel, whom everybody loved
that looked upon her"

Death of a slinky
Natalie Angelone

I watch my slinky somersault down the stairs. Reaching the bottom he plummets to the side. I pick him up and wrap him around my body. I pull the perfect plastic ringlets tightly apart. I dance around in a heavenly tango until I hear a snap. The slinky retracts from my hand in a repulsive urgency and spins ten times around my body to release itself before slapping my other hand. Panic flows in my blood as I pick up his lifeless shape. His tangled limbs are locked like a pair of handcuffs. I start forcefully pulling and pushing the rings inside and outside of each other. "Don't do this to me," I growl. Four hours later my fingers are swollen and burn from the threading through each labyrinth of his death. I stop. The slinky is limp in my lap. I wish he would yell at me, tell me he's mad at me so I could beg for his forgiveness. I wish he would hit me; coil into a python's defense and strike me. But he does nothing. His silent wraps around me and chokes my muffled guilt. But then I think about how he hurt me. I stare at my hand that he slapped. Instead of seeing his body as a link of golden halos', I see they are all hoops of fire that he made me jump through. I lean into all his circles of hell and whisper, "You slut."

"robed"
jane røken

The ghosts are here dancing among the molecules.
They swish dioxide with their robes.
They know how stupid this all is.
So they dance.

— **"Horror"**
Nathan Savin Scott, page 72

Dragging the waters
Annie Neugebauer

"Keep looking!" she screamed
over the wind.
"Keep looking!"
Panic pitched her voice so high
I almost lost it
amidst the waves crashing
just beyond our feet.

"Yeh heard 'er!"
the bearded man bellowed
from my right.
"We drag 'em again!"
and he pulled
his corner of the net
deeper,
me and my corner
trailing with it.

Stillborn
Daniel Romo

I died before birth. My little lungs pleaded for my release. But the umbilical
cord loved me too long; wouldn't let go. I don't remember much. Not the
gagging, gasping. Only the shrieks of my mother. Today she's a steadfast
pillar of guilt. For my birthday she bakes an Angel Food Cake and places it
on my grave. She lights the candles but doesn't blow them out. It would be
a slap to his face. She's convinced the Santa Anas are my premature breath,
and I'm an infant ghost. Full-term breathing haunting her every October.

It was really hot yesterday
Febe Moss

By the afternoon I had died,
my lashes and lids stuck
in a post mortem stink eye.
But like a iron-fisted zombie, I blindly
stalked down the road surrounded by
the devil's promiscuous heat.
I had too much skin, bones, and blood
to surrender to a Texas sun.

In the evening hours like Frankenstein,
I was jolted alive and roamed innocently
under the artificial water. I tried my best

to believe I was an amphibian

in an unnatural world; armies of bubbles
caressed my flesh like a lover
dead set on making my lips wet.
In the tail end of my rebirth,
I came up for air and breathed
victory as the sun fell;
and I watched as the moon
was born out of the clouds.

Mechinopolis
Franklin Murdock

An eclipse can change so much.

The world, with its wall of horizons,
sinks into a desolate posture
truly shocking
by how natural it looks.

The shadow of the cosmos
ubiquitous blanket,
like the pride of Icarus
falls wanting,
willing for something purer,
making promises to God
only to break them
without hesitation, retraction,

attrition.

All nations are one under this
silhouette,
strikingly different than the dreams
uttered by their fathers before them.
Identity lost
Culture, a liability
the individual dies
and Gestalt is born into social gravity.

The land falls silent
and people weep and scream,
murmur ancient words,
cold renditions and recitations
of "eulogy" and "inevitability"
of "threat," "cause," and "effect"
of "deus ex machina"

and they die unburied
in this place,
once a beautiful meadow of ferns

now transubstantiated into monster
from which the creatures,
no longer people,
flee.

Sonnet: connected to each other
Glenn W. Cooper

Connected to each other by synaptic junctions
mediating some simple actions such as whole-body
contraction. Thin rain who are you haunting?
The bowl of congealing cornflakes
on the table is no night to drown in.
"Peace is the heir of dead desire."
A coherent arrangement of objects
The night smoothes out its black tarp
while fatal songs sing to the moon
a dream asleep in the thin rain. A night
to drown in. An unsusual presience.
An approach known as "geometrodynamics".
A dead desire is haunting the thin rain.
Mother, I have not found here what I expected.

Pray for stronger locks
Kimberly Casey

When he fell asleep with closet doors open
he would wake up damaged.
Grind church pews into his knees
and carve his fingertips to steeples unbreakable.
Started sleeping with a bell tower under his pillowcase
hand twisted around the rope at all times.
Rituals patterned their way into bedtime stories
brush your teeth, check the closet
wash your face, check the closet
get pajamas, check the closet
shut off the lights, don't even look at the closet—
hum yourself a cloak, hooded, hide in blankets
and concentrate on breathing.
Every creak of the house speaks of opening doors
erase hinges from existence
pray for stronger locks.
The wolves, cemented statues
on his closet shelves would start to stir,
angry and hungry.

Instant religion
Harry Calhoun

"Belief is clinging; faith is letting go." — *Alan Watts*

walking a dirt road and the light plane
soars heavier than the thin coverlet
of light blue sky over the grave ground

and I think of when I am beneath all this
one with the centuries behind me
unconcerned with the eons ahead

and I begin to fashion a notion
built on the spirits of trees
and the collective consciousness of animal instinct

and in the warm light of day
I weave my own myth
from the fabric of dark sky and stars

one with the centuries behind me
and the eons ahead

Horror
Nathan Savin Scott

We are hiding beneath a faux wood
deck and you are breathing on the off-
beat. I inhale your carbon dioxide

and we recycle fogged air back
and forth between us, the air fired up,
molecules erratic, and together you

and I will suck every last proton out
of this place. This is the place for ghosts,
you tell me, and I cannot argue with you.

The mist between us. The spaces in between.
The other day you inhaled a Camel Light
and blew gray smoke into a grayer sky. The leaves

are dead. My father is dying. The cells
inside him are turning in against themselves,
folding inward like the dough I knead at Papa

John's. I need. One day his cells will pack
it in until there is nowhere to go.
I think about that here with you, under

faux wood, the ground wet beneath us,
the dew. His cells will turn inside and against.
An infinity inward. Sometimes I think

they will collapse into a black hole that sucks
him down into the earth. Other times
I think they will bottle up and then explode.

You are thirteen. I am two years older.
You are white and I am white. The sky is gray.
The ground is wet. These are things I know.

You tell me that you think he is gone.
He isn't. Not yet. We can wait a little longer.

I will keep you warm with my breath.

The ghosts are here dancing among the
molecules. They swish dioxide with their robes.
They know how stupid this all is. So they dance.

I admire them. They delight in their
little world. I laugh and you tell me to shut
the fuck up or he'll hear us.

When you feel fear
Ty Russell

when you feel fear rising
in your throat
crowding out the vast landscape
of your soul
greet him as you would
an old friend
learn from what he has to say
listen
but not too much

then when he turns his back
stab the fucker in the soft spot
between his ribs
choke him
set him on fire
like a den of hibernating snakes
and let the light show you the way

for what is coming
is coming regardless
it's already on its way
we don't need a false messenger
to tell us

Double-feature
Paul McQuade

The stars were splices of film:
flickering out of focus, not there then
not there again in spools of
magnesium. Beneath them,
seared holy into the night:
Gene Vincent,
and The Girl Can't Help It.

It was
malt-shop success at first, of course,
at first, but we needed dialogue
so we talked incoherent into our gin&tonics
    (free-pouring rainwater, a flood of bright lemons)
and smoked, because it was then,
and we did not know

just how poisonous we could be.
Tendrils of smoke rose
into the aether,
mingled with the silver light
until we were coiled,
clasped tight,
in a seaweed of smoke and mirrors.

When you're not you you're the most
you you could ever be
We watched as the scene darkened.
Vincent Price moulded wax.
You screamed, with a shudder,
and your ortolan spine was so damn breakable on the red leather
that I had to bite my tongue to keep from doing it.

Seven ways to conjure the luck of a saltwater sturgeon
Wendy Willis

1. We are obliged
to seek forgiveness
from darkling ghosts
for the backwaters
of what we thought
we thought. 2. A road pitted
with milkweed
and vinca surely ends
in an opaque city,
 a squared-off mayor
& missus can you spare some change?
3. Four white feet
are unlucky
on a racing pony.
Never bet
on a gray. 4. Warning:
A late beer
in a father's hand
can only turn out
badly. 5. You can't warm
to the title widow
without kissing
its round-O mouth
and carrying home
a scrap-purse of stones.
6. Press slow
toward
the milk-sotted morning
for fear of sparrows
and slant-dreams.
7. Set the hook
& spit on the worm
for luck.

Fragments
Robert Vaughan

Can't fathom what possesses
someone to bolt
so suddenly,

disappear

noteless, without warning
signs, surely troubled
but aren't we all...

What urges someone
to leap off a
cliff, fly into a canyon

to be swallowed whole
in fragments

dispersed. Only
one freezing January
month after we'd met.

"believe"
jennifer tomaloff

The stars gave her zero importance. Her soft skin did nothing for the stars. Her exposed breasts made them laugh.

— "Seducing the stars"
Luis Cuauhtemoc Berriozabal, page 81

ISSUE NO. 8

Black cloud snapshots
Andrew J. Stone

"The eyes and the faces all turned themselves toward me, and guiding myself by them, as if by a magical thread, I stepped into the room."
—From the Bell Jar

I. Farewell Lover, Farewell Son

You said the white walls
saved you from his piercing hands
but you were wrong, my
dearest, blood flushed down your
thin thighs as I watched us die

II. Cannibal Lies

She wanted to leave
that's why she killed your son,
why she asked the man
in white to let her die on
the cold operating table

III. Confessions to a Psychologist

I stood there in white
hovering over the limp
flesh below my claws
she was my wife, my dearest,
And how does that make you feel?

The slumbering chair
Chad Redden

and September rains.
His fingers almost rife
with a woman's absence.
A cloud followed him
out into the hallway;
a sound in his ears
for a while. A susurration
about his unmarked grave.

Ghosts don't bleed, period.
Levi Gribbon

She walked up to me and said, "It smells like there is a dead animal in my kitchen."

"Ugh," I responded, "is there?"

She replied, "I hope not. God, I hope not. So far, there is no sign of one."

"You can never be too sure. There might be something living in your room... under your bed, behind your clothes, under your desk, in the vent, in the closet, under the couch... behind the fridge... in some drawer."

"Aaaaah," she shrieked, "stop it's too much too think about!"

I continued ignoring her, "behind the toilet... I always check a toilet before using it. You never know when something is just going to come up and getcha!"

She quickly changed the subject, "we have a huge red ring in the toilet water now. It's gross."

"From... from... vaginas?"

"NOOOOO!" she yelled, "I have no idea."

"Then... from what?"

"Honestly, I'm thinking the ghost has something to do with this. Ghost vagina?"

"Ghost vag, most def."

Skits
Joshua Otto

Once upon a time, there was one who gave up remembering
and became divisible. Long before that, another once had
explained the limited utility of one's telling in detailed,
cotidian scenarios: Laughing, don't quit yet, I'm counting on you.

I cannot make promises without spilling regrets.

On such beaches, musical waves are spelt to die. Who
is willing to sing with such heart? Through the smoke of a pipe
I see your silhouette pinned to the wrist of the melody.
Every geography is mapped in the record of your voice.

Night at the sick hotel
Howie Good

1

A famous man's youngest daughter, tormented by visions of burning airships, trips the metal detector. I feel like an empty gray glove. Strangers crowd into the elevator with us. Only later do they think to ask if we're going down. The weather has turned. Buds pop, a nation of suicide bombers in dynamite vests.

2

Hear that? A low wailing? Like a tornado of meat flies? I must have signed my name in the wrong place or acquired the wrong kind of expertise. As I drive into town, the glass eye soaks overnight in a glass of wine. No one among my so-called friends volunteers to save me. There used to be a rule, Monstrous face, monstrous soul. The crow furiously pecking at something red in the road ignores it.

3

I make a cup of my heart, what should not be but is, the cloud shapes like accusations increasingly hard to dispute. A pornomaniac has been nailed to the cross among the agitators and shoplifters. Why take sides when it could not not be? Love thy neighbor, the homeless man under the stadium says, communicating with obscene gestures rather than words.

The exodus
Michael Bagwell

Everyone is leaving. They walk in pensive lines
with each eye under the falling feet of those
in front and each hand grasping
bulky sacks of food and clothing.
Dirt lies thick on their fingers like continents
afloat on oceans of skin.

I watch them go from the shore.
No one else lingers there, or even looks.
Just rocks and sand, water and the remnants of stars.
The windowed faces of the buildings
are like arachnids with their legs torn off.
The whole of the countryside looks like some damaged,
monstrous beast that, perhaps once, had been beautiful.

Even the wild dogs are leaving now,
paddling hopelessly out to sea
so as not to die in this place.

Yet I stay and when the last ship sails
and the last bird takes flight,
I walk back to my home,
keeping the sea at my back.

Seducing the stars
Luis Cuauhtemoc Berriozabal

She wanted to seduce the stars.
Being able to fly she was able
to hover right under them.
But the stars paid no mind to her
exhibition. She began to blow
her nose, pretending to cry.
Her breath was heavy. The stars
gave her zero importance. Her
soft skin did nothing for the stars.
Her exposed breasts made them laugh.

Hiroshima
Margaret Emma Brandl

And when it was all said and done,
We hurled ourselves through the night streets,
Howling to the moat of a darkened castle,
Slogging through mud and past bright white gas stations.
In a dark room with candy colors
We screamed our lungs out, gorging on sugared soda and
ice cream.
We leaned into each other. We grasped for things.
We dragged ourselves down pathways.
And our whispered conversations were carried on the wind
Away from our ears,
And our morning's memories came back into our hearts

It was midnight, and then it was not.
Sharp winds stung at eyes that would not cry tears
Even staring at that stone skeleton lit
Beyond a tongue of flame reflected in waters and stones,
So beautiful, so beautiful,
So quiet,
And there we were.

Blob
Matthew Harrison

Its image could be anything.

You get the picture. It burns

with atmosphere. It lives, consumes

consumers like cinema, a radiant

blood bag for donors big, then bigger

to a mass crave. You stomach it.

To end it you think incineration,

but only a slow freeze will do.

You know, says a cool boy

to constellations. He looks away

from the girl behind the house

in Hollywood. *You know,*

plenty of people with their right minds

thought they saw things that didn't exist.

He thinks of what could be, innocent

as crickets in the backyard. The parents

stay asleep. The girl is just there. The star system

implies her. *You know, like flying saucers,*

the light just right in the angle of imagination.

He turns and takes her in, alert

with common craving, a blob

soon to be. His monstrous heart beats

in a drive-in B movie. Give in to it,

and you grow with horrifying romance.

And if that is what it is, then

this is just an ordinary night.

Pushed off the blues train
Melanie Browne

I start haunting the tracks,
a woman drinks May Wine
over my grave,
it starts to rain,
sometimes people
want to take pictures,
but I never smile,
that would be rude,
I am
floating in front
of the sleeper car
where he first
seduced me,
softly singing
Guthries' 'Last Train',
and now the rain
has stopped,
the woman staggers
towards her house,
clutching at her heart

This is Stephen
Peter Taylor

And if you had ceased that day
I would not have seen you
Here and understood
The intimate cynicism of the world.
  — Don Coles

I

We all end on a slab somewhere
open pages from Gray's Anatomy
smelling of ether and formaldehyde
the final invasion
coming too late

your body
did not wait
for surgeons and accidents

its pallid strength
spiteful of itself
yet calm
in its resolution
to remain an enigma

a bruised print

Brother, where are you?

II

Time

changed you into ceremonies
kept the others sane

my heart
shrunk to a fist
with the slow agony

of recognition

from
the moment
I entered that room
until the moment
I exit this

my visitations

between earth
which holds you
and thought
in which you exist

III

Midnight faces
explode

the firemen I called
knowing they respond faster
helmets firecoats boots
hunched in that basement room

coroner in evening dress
a piece of confetti on his collar
squeezes in
one more body between
cocktails and a nightcap

instructing the police
to drive my sister and I
over to tell your wife
and children

we buy coffee and doughnuts on the
way

IV

I think of dying every day

slow excretion of self
endless form of heart
brain kidneys tiny
explosions
waiting to expose the film

I keep your pictures safe
from the infinite exposure
of the sun

when I advance the roll
you disappear

last frame
carrying your ashes
in a box

surprised
how little is left

V

A cold grimace
all you left to the world
and what to me?

tongue swollen as scream
face a pale mask
orbiting
my night constellation

hand stretches
to touch you
across film across thought
tearing illusive
filaments of memory

language contaminates
as it creates

the flawed universe
we imagine and inhabit

turning the print
over and over
in my mind

The blue whale phenomenon
Steve Castro

The blue whale that fell from the sky,
Shattered through steel, concrete and
Disappeared into a sea of chaos and destruction.
The helicopter's cable snapped — the ensuing
Explosion was a firework display of technological
Failure colliding with a mountain — if the pilot had
Lived, the whole world would have called him
"The human impossibility." I would have called him
Jonah — If I lived in Alaska, I would be rich because
I would open the first blue whale and grits restaurant.
I would sell a liter of vodka in a blue plastic bucket and
Throw a shard of a blue whale's tooth inside it and call my drink
"The one of a kind special." I would sell blue whale ribs,
Blue whale cheese burgers and blue whale steaks with
Eskimo pies served by cute Eskimo girls in bikinis — I would sell
Coca cola with coca leaf straws. I would also sell
French fries made by a real French chef who I would
Convince to move to Alaska for six months out of the year
In exchange for as many blue whale tongues as
He can sell to the Parisian bourgeois — Of course all the
Blue whale meat would be brought to me by
Massive trucks — Helicopters and their faulty cables
Would be banned from my establishment within a
Two mile radius — unless of course "the human impossibility"
Was seen walking up my restaurant's massive ivory steps

The birds
Walter Conley

that chirp is
electric, e-
lectronic and
subsonic
shot
like bullets from
a twenty-two
aimed at
me and you

now you clearly
hear it too
so
why pretend
that I am crazy
we
both know
that we will do
what
unseen
metal god-birds
tell us to

ISSUE NO. 9

when I
grow up,
I want to
eat the
weak.

DINOSAURS OF EMF

"when i grow up"
megan kennedy

*I thought I said love. Maybe
I said death.*

— "The small death"
Erin Croy, page 89

The small death
Erin Croy

I thought I said love. Maybe
I said death.

I have only been speaking
this incomprehensible language now
nearly three decades. Maybe longer.
It is worse than German.

I should grow used
to it like the tree along my street
with three split tops. It could not decide
which sun to go toward. You do not know it;
you have never been here.

I think it is a blue spruce
like the one I was taller-than, then
not-taller-than, in my parent's yard,
because the needles have a blue cast
like a heart.

Do you understand me
if I say when you broke
all those dishes,
I would have minded neither
the shards in my back,
nor the scars?

I have had some thoughts this morning.

Maura
Eamonn Lorigan

And when I realized
we would never make love
again
it was like looking
at all the broken windows in
New York.

Ribcage
Dawn Schout

The cold sky has no life
in it tonight,
as if it too is dying
with sycamore leaves.
Cirrus clouds form a ribcage
over the moon.
The sky's heart
glows ghostly white.

The alien invasion tapes, #87
Dorene O'Brien

It was back in '63 they set down in my field,
and I was too damn angry to be scared.
I knew that crop was gone and it wasn't a thing I could do about it.
When they come out of their spaceship—
no, no it wasn't a door that swung down like on a castle,
but a giant car door, like on my Buick?—
they come out, three of 'em no taller than my knee,
and just stared at me, no expression in those big glassy eyes,
no sorrow for what they done to my field.
"We come in peace," they said without sayin' it out loud
but I heard it in my head
and I looked at my flattened, withered wheat and said, "The hell you do."
Have you ever seen mangled wheat, the stalks cracked, the feathers singed?
A whole season: It's enough to make you cry. And I did.
Standin' in the middle of my broken field with those three aliens, wellin' up,
the door to their giant ship propped open,
a sickening light pourin' from inside
and slicin' across my barren field like a knife.
They do somethin' like rock, paper, scissors and one comes over and tells me
I'm supposed to be some kind of alien ambassador.
100 acres, gone, the exhaust from their craft fellin' my crop like a tornado,
the shoots fallin' like dominoes, like ambushed soldiers,
the stink latchin' onto my nostrils.
"You fellas best be on your way," I said as patiently as any man who just lost his
livelihood can, and for the first time they look around.
Sure I think they're doin' damage assessment,
conjurin' a way to bring the wheat back,
and I picture those fuzzy stalks risin'
like an army of mini Lazaruses across the dead plain,
work hard to send that image to them with my mind.
But they're fixed on somethin' else now, and it's Tessie, comin' toward us,
haunch-slow, jaws workin', wheat cracklin' beneath her bovine hooves.
I point to her, my prize heifer, shake my head and give them a firm "NO!"
But Tessie and the aliens, they're starin' at one another, stock still, hypnotized.
Even today I wonder what they said that made her walk right past me,
through the blade of sharp light and into that shiny crop killin' machine:
You'll be happier with us, He don't appreciate you, YOU are the true alien
ambassador.

So that's how I lost my wheat and my cow in the same hour.

The man from the insurance company don't believe me, but I know you do.
You see this stuff all the time, so I was hopin' you could talk to 'im,
tell 'im about the giant car door, the two-foot Martians, a prized cow that
trundled, hooves clickin', into another dimension.

Arkansas
Kimberly Casey

I found your body while barefoot in the marsh,
tossed like a candy wrapper on the ground
crumpled and worn from rainwater dripping.
I scooped you up like beach sand in my palms
and pressed you to my ear, listening to the
absence of air in your chest, the hollow loss
of something not yet understood
Your shoulders were still bleeding
the brightest red of sunset
catching the kindling of your bones.
Tonight I will take you home
crack your chest plate with precision
and explore the inside of your shell myself,
picking tiny diamonds from your bloodstream
using needles like chopsticks
cleaning your caverns of all things unnatural
Then stitch you up, create a nest in the ground
grind a gravestone from granite –
I'll never tell them where you are buried,
upside down under tree roots,
flying weightlessly home.

Un-interpreted dream (4)
Kate Frank

I am holding the door shut.
Someone, a boy I loved, is helping me
hold it shut but he is also not
there & I am alone in the room.
The room is both the safest place
I can be because I am hidden,
& also the least safe because
I am trapped & they are coming & when
they come & I cannot hold them
there will be nowhere else to go.
I am not dead yet but I know
I am dead. It is inevitable.
The boy's face is at once pock-
marked & smooth, his hair is at once
a stiff mohawk & an army crew cut.
His name is Conner & he eats
an apple while he leans against
the door. It is such an innocuous hallway.
My pursuers were not so frightening
until they were. Conner puts his shoulder
to the door, which is now bulging,
pulsing with the force of my enemies
& he turns his face toward me
with his shoulder still against the door
& smiles like a pirate, rogue-ish, or like
he genuinely loves me & time stops
& starts over in a loop of his head
turning & the enemies pulsing &
his smile growing & frozen on his face.

My greatest accomplishment
Matthew Byrne

It began in the living room.
An orange, overgrown puppet
would say "You have ten seconds
to get to your parents' room."
Trying to run was like wading
through molasses. Trying
to scream yielded only a whisper.
I felt his grimace on my back.
I'd wake just before he counted
to ten, drenched in sweat,
clenching the blanket,
shouting for my mother.
One night I decided I'd had enough.
He started in but I dragged him
by the throat to the bathroom,
and flushed him down the toilet.
That was that for years, until
one night he paid his last visit.
He stabbed me with a rubber knife,
and we laughed like two old pals.

Ghost tears
Paul Hellweg

I shed ghost tears
all day long and
in my sleep.
No coward I,
yet fear
keeps me
and so many others
adrift in solitude
and silence, telling
our own truths
to no one
but ourselves.

The black
Meaghan Ford

I have had so many lovers.
—half the world!
My name sighing out of their throats.
Yersinia Pestis,
Little safety pin,
The Great Plague

I was kisses traveling on the wings on fleas
The coats of rats
The softest taste of metal in their mouths.
Before they even knew what I was they were in my arms.

My beautiful children
Such frail, peach blushing skin
It was begging to be canvas
Screaming out for the stroke of my hands

I couldn't help myself.
My mark is all
Over you
Blooming with black bruises from all the times we touched
Sun kissed freckles and rings of fever flush
The blood curdling in your stomach

I loved you like the spring
Like you were all the warm days I never knew
Gripped knee shivering in cargo holds
For the promise of a new world.

I am a song on the lips of children in a school yard
The echo of wood wheel'd carts as they groan through your streets
A wrist smelling like dried flowers at your bedside
The last stunted gasp your body will twitch with
The blanket they will wrap you in
And never let you go.

Dear November,
Robert McDonald

It's strange to think of you today, when the crocuses
bloom
on a lawn decked with snow. But the grand
blossoming
is not yet come, and the sky

if it had its way
might declare "never," might call
for sleet,
for snow, for northern wind.
November

frosts the icy glass
of the April day,
and arrests
the slow greening
of the lawn.

November
would push
every bud back
into the earth.
We might long for wings.

We might dream
we are ravens. Even
a wicked heart
will love
the stained world.

The sky darkens, the snow
becomes
a dance,
and every ballerina
beautifully falls.

Smashed ghazal
Sarah J. Sloat

My intentions start wholesome my intentions
intend to blend with the rain on the roof
mean to scatter like badland hares
tonight

The plumbing gets busted
the faucet unstoppers its nose

a mind may be open a mind
may be wormholed and closed for repairs tonight

Planet of surrealistic painters. Planet of spanish. Planet of snakes and apes
and plaintalkers who'll feast on veal and pears tonight

Staggering with enormous adornment, the broomstick implodes:
the straw chokes with cherries
the pole rolls into a cellar replete
with tobacco and roses

where wine bottles
left uncorked seep in their lairs tonight
The ship lists and canters; waves dig wells from the flotsam

the damned captain laughs, unhinged
and unawares tonight. It wasn't my fault. I was only

lolling about, oily, bashing the masters
of maritime art, plugging round
squares with holes

in the gallery aisle
it doesn't storm but it pours, O
one single raindrop travels

the stairs
tonight.

Ufology
Susie Swanton

One summer every night on the back porch I read books
and next door my neighbor would slam the back door,
light a cigarette, and sit down.
He sometimes took out what looked like a black fabric pencil case
and from that a needle, tap it, and jab it
into his thigh, right through his jeans.

The aliens flew low those nights
to take him up the tractor beam.
He never went all the way, not into the ship.

He hung in the sky as deep
gold in the streetlights
as my dad's capped tooth.
"That's not me,"
he'd say pointing to himself in the air
while still sitting in a lawn chair on the deck,
watching his body turn slowly
as he turned slowly to me.
"That's not me. I'm not like that."
He hung quiet, and he'd sit quiet on their back porch,
staring at me while I read
The Martian Chronicles or The Three Stigmata of Palmer Eldritch.

And what was it like to be as old as 19, I wondered,
what could his parents think, how could his mother hate him.
He always loudly whispered,
"That's not me, this isn't me,"
as his body rotated in the force field.
Every dig of the needle his body moved closer
to the belly of the ship.
"I'm not doing this. Only my hands are.
These hands aren't even mine."

Another light
Wesley Dylan Gray

The echoing haunt
of breaking waves
cringe upon the verge
of this world
and the next,
rising to the
tower,

white stone
bleached from
wind and sea and salt,
into the eye
whose light reaches
cresting depths
where Lost Ones
lie in dripping graves,
to fill saddened ears
dwelling upon the loss.

And when Moon staggers in,
wipes its feet upon the mat,
another light is seen
at aberrant angles
from the rocks,
finding form
in lamenting figure,
bleeding, glowing,
bleeding, glowing—
searching for home.

—the spade pecking at itself
till all that's left to eat
is the dampness in its bones.

— *"* * *"*
Simon Perchik, page 111

ISSUE NO. 10

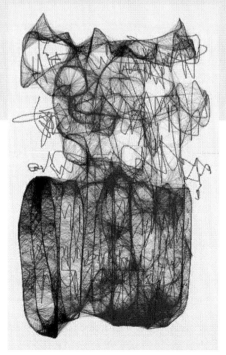

"#12"
keith higginbotham

Note: This issue's artwork was
submitted in collaboration with
David Tomaloff's poem, also
featured in this issue.

Loup garou i-iii {a suite}
David Tomaloff

i. LYCANTHROPE

hyper
werewolf

; soft it was
, the city sliding

off its back

a man can only
be a man except

in those rare cases
when he is more

ii. VARIATIONS ON A THEME

some cities are cities
; other cities are fires

the undead of the forests
that preceded them

still inhabit the cracks
, where they live

on the gin
& the blood

of the living

we count the days
by the stars that pass

; we forget what we can
by the blue light of day

iii. AMONG/AMUCK

the sharpened teeth
; the shoulders

sometimes
, she said
, I fear for the worst

Mad mother's lullaby

Caroline Misner

Hush, hush, sweet baby boy,
not a word must you utter.
Shut your eyes against the night,
without you the night would be much better.

You diminish me, sweet child, bit by bit;
fragments of a broken puzzle
that never seem to fit.

Keep quiet, my love
and don't say a word.
Hush, hush, sweet baby;
you don't want to be heard.

A creature of silence and sometimes of sound;
if not for you, sweet baby,
I wouldn't stay around.

Hush, hush, sweet baby boy,
not a sound must you utter.
If you were dead right now,
my life would be much better.

Mother tomorrow and mother today.
Hush, hush, sweet baby
and please go away.

Voraginous wounds
Drea Jane Kato

What I want is not anything
offered here. What I want
is jeweled red horses, chains
connecting all my organs,
a mangled music box heart.

Reality is destroying me
and something great
is seeping out
through my veins.
I inhale the smoke
and accept things as they are.
It is officially dissolved.
Promises, promises..

What I want is a nostalgia
like acid burning holes in me.
What I want is angels reaching down
from their delicate ether palace,
touching me underneath my clothes.

What I want is a mosquito net
to choke you with
and a pond to toss you in after.
What I want is to watch
a river of mucus float by
filled with fish that dance
and light up like
little balls of hope.

I want the air to smell like
candy and animal flesh and coffee.
I want to see rainbows every day.
What I want is every president's
head on a platter. What I want is

to eat and drink and have sex
like everyone but I can't.

What I want is to live in crystal castles
and her death; I imagine it sounding
like velcro, then a weak
almost inaudible sound.

What I want is to pull a trigger
that pulls a million triggers,
a watermelon scent in the brain,
a sunflower field, additional siblings.

What I want is trash in my veins,
every single person walking down the
street
sane and well and
sex with cake.

Her, gone, 3 A.M.
Harry Calhoun

Woke in the middle of a hard starless night,
all dark in the bedroom and chilly cold outside.

I could almost hear the tubercular darkness
coughing hemorrhage. It had gone so wrong

with her death to my presence.
The slimmest moon will not spit its shadow

onto the wall of her absence. Once the gibbous
lit our way into and out of the shadows,

but now the wolf has its way, creeping
into our old backyard and your new savage wanderlust.

My old faithful dog and I do not like this.
We are not timid but there is much to fear,

waking to bland black water pressing
with the quiet suffocation of loneliness from all sides.

The void with her gone crackles between my ears,
white noise in the radio receiver of the mind.

I place my body like a slovenly bookmark,
a poor offering between the sheets where we

used to sleep. Hope to pick up some wreckage of rest,
adrift on the beach of a hard starless night.

See stitches
Nazifa Islam

I'll slit my throat in front of you.
Watch me. Slitting wrists is only done
in private but I'll draw the knife
across my jugular in front of you
and a mirror if that's your demand.
I'm not shy. I'll strip naked first
if you prefer. I'll light my clothes
on fire and try to cover myself
in the ashes. It won't work but I'll do it.
You'll see how stubborn I can be.
You'll see mania. You'll get acquainted
with blood. I'll make your dreams
nightmares – that's what I'm here for.
Why the hell are you laughing?

Rêve à la gauche
Jennifer Lobaugh

I dreamed with my head to the left last night
cheek pressed soft into the pillow
my breath hot, and even as time
my mind an unkempt garden

I heard your voice through a tunnel of light
beckoning from times long past
        Remember when?
you used to speak in polygons
and the lies were kinder then

I saw an Easter morning, starchy white
Sunday drowsy, Sunday clean
it was stereophonic violet
a heartbreak in a dream

Sarah's inside sarah
John Grey

When they called
the girl Sarah,
they didn't know
they were creating
another Sarah,
a body within
hers waiting for
the name to latch onto,
to slide inside
in a fist of clear light
and grow as the outside grew,
but deadlier, darker.

When she bloomed
into a lissome beauty,
blonde as a captured sun,
the shadowy brunette
was already too large for her cage
and scratched against the pink wall
with a dagger.

And when the man whispered
in a delicate pink ear,
"Sarah, Sarah",
the hidden one would
leap out and shower
him with the kisses
of her singing blade.

Scarrings
Jack Hodil

Which is worse,
the girl who
cries after the abortion
or the girl who
does not?

They will both be eaten
by the same god, after all,
despite how well they may
walk through their respective mazes.

Sometimes the shortest of distances
can be the most overwhelming,
with bodies that have grown too full
to be carried any further.

These are the things that only
happen when nothing else can.
Like a stabbing,
you won't feel it until
they have already taken it out.

Gathering
Lauren D.M. Smith

Yellow eyes,

Slit pupils,

Stare out from the darkness

Leaves that rustle,

Shadows twitch,

No winds blow through the night

Escaping,

Clouds move past,

The sliver moon appears

A bright line

In dark sky,

The reverse of those eyes

Tail swishes slowly,

The eyes stare,

The cat watches you move

Another cat,

And another

Come to sit, staring at you

Glowing eyes,

Stepping back,

The cats follow you

Turning back,

You move away,

Only to find more cats

Up in the skeleton

Trees, and on

The roofs of the abandoned houses

The cats gaze

Down at you,

Silhouetted against the night.

Bushes rustle,

Cats there too.

On the path, claws gouging the earth.

Shining bright,

Against the dark,

A curved menace, hidden by fur.

Everywhere

Yellow eyes

Staring straight into you

No escape,

Surrounded,

They slink slowly forward...

Poem for a poet
Kirby Wright

These days I find blood
In strange places,

Drops falling like rain
Staining the carpet.

I remember the razor dragging,
Unzipping me from myself.

Why do I plant
The arms and legs of dolls

In the earth
Of the redwood planter?

It amuses you.
I know.

Am I planting myself?
My only pictures of you

Are on the flaps of books.
You search for women

To belong to
When you know, deep down,

You belong to me
Or at least the part of me

That makes you hunger
For more bloody morsels.

The night I realized I'd long ago lost my son
Nancy Flynn

hemoglobin red   most lurid hue

that scar

come by   one night in the 90s   riding your no-light bike

smashed   a month until 20   Monday night football

(Jello shots?)   how does it happen?   what

makes a boy fly   into a car?

windshield crystals   slicing through lip

not a look   you desire   in a family photo

to this day   turning   angles that restore

your face   leading man   (empirical)

low-pitch rumble   your voice   ramped-up

toward jarred   gangland sweet   that summer

every hoop court   tar-taped   nothing

patched, only play   never the payday   always

hazard hazard hazard

postures   potholes   pop/guns

how near   a face can get   and yet

the maximum   son in the flesh

(after he's tanned it forever)

why didn't it peel?   because mothers

cling like lichen   swab the rash

tweeze the miniscule grit

eviscerating   the high-beam glare

inside   then sinking   no, sunk

my sorry   love-shot stone

your boyish lostness

what did you feel   behind your matte mask

tethering to gauze   who's dissing you   ugly?

she tries to recall the ranting

in the emergency room

from his drunken   mangled mouth

instead that echo

the man in the car   who cried

Did I kill him?

Nightmare radio report
Walt Garner

"A Mister Thomas Bliss of Stonington
is missing and presumed dead this morning.
He was taken from his home at knife point
by a roving gang of motorcyclists
police have had no luck in apprehending.
Four other men in Bliss's walk of life
(he teaches at the elementary school)
have disappeared from their Connecticut
homes in identical circumstances
(they were taken while reading Robert Frost).
By the morning after the abductions
the previous four were found in pieces,
their skulls having been hollowed out, their ribs
gnawed on and showing signs of being boiled
to extract the marrow for soup or stew
these renegades, cannibals, murderers
create to shore up strength for ensuing crimes.
Police have found what they can only call—
ghoulish as it sounds— 'belly sentences,'
which they think Mister Bliss in writhing wrote
upon the ground surrounding their infernal
campfire. (The Palmer Method was employed.)"

" 'Plato laughs and cracks a bone across
his knee; Demosthenes drinks Southern Comfort
from a skull. Gnawing on a bloody arm,
Aurelius is watching as I write
these words. They've killed four teachers just like me.
If you can't save me, you need to know
their names and ways so you can stop their run
of rampaging through the ranks of men who
teach at the elementary level.' "

"The police surmise the captors watching
Bliss wriggle like a worm in the outer edges
of the firelight would not have known
that he was communicating with the law
enforcement community, but instead

they'd ascribe his worming to timidity,
self-pity, cowardice, lack of manhood.
But what he wrote in man-sized worm castings
amounts to an indictment the D. A.
only needs to write in legal jargon.
Bliss named names in his belly sentences
that'll put this gang away for good."

*

Simon Perchik

I dig this grave
the way migrating birds
remember the exact site
—the spade pecking at itself
till all that's left to eat
is the dampness in its bones.

It took this crow forever, first
to darken, then
to fly but I am still afraid
keep widening this hole
not sure —all night each star
returning to the same spot
and this blade somehow heavier.

I lay down a bird
that still has wings
has a place you can use —the air
is not so safe anymore
and the dirt against its body
already growing into light

into some great mountain range
and these few feathers around it waist
looking all over for you

—you are always falling into rivers
—what you breathe now
comes from these shallow graves
emptied then filled —this crow
with its back to the sky
and no room left on Earth.

*Little ones, your time would be
better spent keeping this in mind:
the mouth of a demon
is hardly the kind of place
you want to go throwing dirt.*

*You might stir up a hunger
for your own bones.*

— **"Slither."**
Georgie Delgado, page 118

"neighbors"
eryk s. wenziak

Mermaids
Holly Day

we were going to take the boat out, sail
to the edge of the world, tease
the monsters waiting there with out
bare, dangling feet, toes tickling the ocean skin
like tiny pink fish

but you had to go and ruin it
chase shore-hugging mermaids instead
had to search clam-shell bikinis for pearls
find out where baby mermaids come from

we were going to become pirates
treasure hunters, world explorers
wrestle giant squid at the world's edge
find the fountain of youth

but you had to go and spoil everything
in your search for suburban normalcy
chase dreams of apron-clad mermaids
who'd give up their kingdoms for you.

Red water
Michael Andrew

all dennis wanted to do was eat burritos but he was stuck watching the
livestock by the time he got to the field they were madly walking in circles
bellowing by mid-afternoon their urine had turned red and purple last year
the hills around his farm had been transformed into translucent triangles and
polyhedrons he wondered if this could be the cause of his animal's illness

Wolf
Amy Elisabeth Olson

wolf 1

when he visited me last
night he left me
with three black hairs.

each one he said
would allow me to change
a moment past. with a wood
match i lit one on fire
and inhaled the thickness of burning
hair. with a bone needle i wove
the other into a ball of yellow
yarn. i spent four days knitting
a scarf and wore it instead
around my waist. i pressed the
third hair across my tongue and
let it stick between two
teeth. when i woke up this morning
it was there, still. i am sure
it will never not be.

wolf 2

i yellowed together the wolf-worn
tatters, gathering wool and teething
apart patches. the blunted scissor
legs clasping together fabrics long
left in willowed grasses.

you left me pausing
and watering, you left me
wolfing and sallow. maybe not as
edgeless as to seam, but you left me
much more toothy than green.

wolf 3

from the no
rth the win

d floated

to me a how
l. i under
stood i

t to be a sign

that my tend
er predator was still the
re, though no
t haunting me any

more with his teeth,

anymore with his hair.

My greatest fear
Brad Liening

It's hard to tell what the greater fear is:
to be discovered or no one caring
to discover you. A holy man
thinks about it for a long time.
The earth trembles, sending up a few ghosts
while others fall into brand-new chasms.
In a century or two, people will ride
donkeys down into the now-old
chasms on tours to ooh and aah
and be bitten by poisonous snakes.
Some poisonous snakes roost in the sky
and are incorrectly identified as clouds.
Someday they will drop to earth and
it will be horrible. It's my greatest fear.

Womanslaughter
Gale Acuff

Miss Hooker died last night, I dreamt. She's my
Sunday School teacher but, last night, no more,
she didn't see the Mack that had no lights
and I was driving it, I want to be
a truckdriver when I grow up, I'm just
9 now to her 25 or so, she's

old, or was, and I want to marry her,
or did, but now I can't, not just in real
life but in dreams, too, unless she comes
back to life for me tonight and I hope
she isn't angry and forgives me, like
Jesus does, or she said He does—unless

I'm so sinful that I'm sent to Hell, where
I'll live an eternity of torment,
not that I don't deserve it, I cheated
on my last math test and flunked anyway,
though to my credit not by very much,
but that's sin for you, it only takes some

and not a lot to sink you into fire.
And to my credit again, in last night's
dream I called the cops and turned myself in:
Yes, it was an accident, I said, *but
I knew better than to drive without lights
after dark, and, no, I wasn't drinking
and you can test me.* They did and I passed
so that's something. Boy, was her family

steamed at me, who can blame them, and wouldn't
let me attend the funeral, and then
I went to court and pleaded guilty, which
was the least I could do though it didn't
bring Miss Hooker back. They executed
me but it only hurt a second and
then I guess I went to Hell but—holy
moley—I woke up this morning alive

and dressed for Sunday School but was shaking
so much I couldn't straighten my clip-on
bow tie and wound up with it on upside
down but never noticed 'til Miss Hooker
told me after class and fixed it for me,
her fingers at my throat and all her grace.

Getting up to meet yourself coming down
Rick Bailey

A man wakes in the middle of the night and discovers his head is on fire.
His wife sleeps beside him, exhausted from years of childbirth, the daily
work of children, hearth and home. He knows better than to wake her or
burn her nice pillow cases. He slips out of bed and stands in front of the
mirror. It's such a big one, he whispers, more than enough. He tamps out his
sideburns, confining the flames to the top, then pulls back the curtains, opens
the window, and climbs out on the roof. Above their silver maple, the moon
is a giant cookie. Damp under his bare feet, the brittle shingles scratch and
tick as he crawls toward top of the house. He is a torch. Tonight he could be
a meteor. He could dive to earth and make a crater that would fill with cool
water. His remains, mere crumbs, would puzzle scientists from around the
world for years. Beneath him, his children roll in their beds with dreams of
their own. His wife turns toward his place, inhales, exhales, and rests an arm
where his chest should be. When he reaches the chimney, he rests his back
against it and waits, grateful for the warmth of the brick. A breeze brings the
smell of apples already starting to drop. He can't see much after all. Now
what, he wonders. And why.

Slither.
Georgie Delgado

You can't imagine the ease
with which we travel between towns
when none of your angry sword-
swingers
remember to check the swamps.

Each one grows fat with our kind.
The mountains, too. At night,

we have often been mistaken
for high-rising trees, swaying
in the wind outside those caves
where even the oracles would lose
themselves amidst our undying.

Every life we enter
ends the same way:

screaming
fracturing
clanging
fire

and so we slither on, watching
all the little children being spun
god yarns in the comfort of bed,
"If you throw dirt into the hydra's
mouth, all its teeth turn into skeletons."

We have wondered at times
how it would feel to exist in a place
where that sort of thing was the truth.

and it is more difficult to believe in
with every passing year,
with every new pond of gore
left burning white hot and acidic.

Little ones, your time would be
better spent keeping this in mind:
the mouth of a demon
is hardly the kind of place
you want to go throwing dirt.

You might stir up a hunger
for your own bones.

You are my sunshine

F.J. Bergmann

You held my gaze a second too long.
You were smiling when you didn't mean it.
I thought I heard you say my name
in a conversation with another woman.
When the moon waned with the year,
I felt threatened,

so I left the letters on your desk, written with
a Rapidograph filled with blood (mine)
and an anti-coagulant; unsigned,
because I knew that you knew.

I sent you the nesting marquetry boxes
containing dried poppies and a grackle skull.
I nailed maimed homunculi braided from black grass
to the outside of your house at points corresponding
to the six cardinalities, where you will never find them.

No translation should have been necessary
but you did not acknowledge or apologize
so I entered your dark house while you were
asleep and hid behind a large rock
and met you less than halfway up the mountain
as you trudged back home from the valley of night.

A series of short poems about the Chinese Invasion (1952)

Simon Jacobs

I. "This Ain't No Land of the Rising Sun"

Cyclical,
the revolutions,
& where they started
under oppressive scorching heat
at the beginning of the day.

II. "Rare New Forms of Bacteria"

An old newspaper
brown & faded with age
reads, as if hysterical satire:
"Beware the Eastern Threat!"
If only we'd known.

III. "Vestigial Organs"

The words "puppet state,"
said over breakfast,
conjured gruesome images of split-armed marionettes
come to snatch boys like me & take them away
in airships.

IV. "No-Fly Zones"

A solitary zeppelin
purring on the orange horizon,
nosing gently at the air,
a slothful, harmless animal,
pouring leaden death from above.

V. "Everything Was Clear for a Moment in Time"

Communication standstill,
stealth planes only
creeping metaphorical tides of red.

Until they weren't.

VI. "Pachysandra in the Atomic Garden"

For the sake of diplomacy
negotiations failed.
For the sake of peace
they went to war.

VII. "Maoist Punks Are the Worst!"

Banners painted thick with crude portraits and slogans.
The rain doesn't dissolve the paint—
curiously, the water cannon does.

VIII. "Traces of Black Magic"

He always knew
when the trains had just left the station;
slick concrete, where the steam condensed,
or red flags flickering in the distance.

IX. "Victorian Futurism"

My grandfather said, "We could go underwater,"
my father said we didn't have the means.
My grandfather replied by unrolling a dusty set of blueprints;
a machine to take us there, he said.

The girl whose face is in faux porcelain bowls
Tammy Ho Lai-Ming

She makes no apologies. Full of sleep,
Her subtle rudeness is no one else's responsibility.
You believe that she's sweet. She smiles, she nods,
She says Yes. She's most certainly not listening.
She's fantasising about Indian clouds, Polish maps,
Dead magazines on French desks.

She makes no apologies. She reads and reads
Whole night long like a hypnotised sheep.

She makes no apologies. Her bizarre upturned lamps
Littered in her house are like grail cups. They hold
Solidified drops of past and present love.

She makes no apologies. Any indulgences
For her are necessities. Three coffees
Before sex just so she burps caffeine
After sighing: Go deeper. Go deep.

She makes no apologies. Call her a Cambodian
And she laughs. Call her an 'authentic' Chinese
She would flinch. Where's her cheongsam?

She makes no apologies. The only spontaneous
Things she does are motivated by changing status
Of consciousness, but more often, body fluids:
'Creative juice is selective about lying.'

No apologies.

Two magpies
Walter Bjorkman

mourn as one, chanting barn cackles from empty lofts. Outside, night woods choruses echo their sympathy. Paint my neck yellows, crimson and green, I scratch — bleed it black, I no longer feel. Lie forever on your side, I will bring tufted grass to your lips, you will not eat. Every seven years I move the soil atop your body, my withered arms turn over your bones. Left alone, they would never stir.

Absence
Vanessa Young

It has been a while
since you explained
time as a dream,
a collective trick
made to deceive
me from believing
that I am at once
the child, wild curls
in the breeze,
and the old woman
I have never seen.
It has been a while
and it never shall be.

Winter solstice 2010
Thomas Piekarski

The old unseen serpent swallows up the stars.   — *Anne Sexton*

1.

The moon eclipsed two nights ago,
Went full the following night.
Everywhere. This time it cries.

Swarmed by battalions of extinct fish
That inky sediment infiltrates its scales,
Mantis, Mantra, Manhattan.

Winter solstice yesterday, light shut down.
Squid squirt ink darker than deepmost
Disconsolate sea cisterns.

Licentious: Libyan land grab gluts headlines.
To avoid wavering amid unnerving quietude
Axis shifts onto men's worm-eaten

Flesh piled high to be burnt within the hour.

2.

The bellicose rhythm of Lonely Hearts Club
Is no idiom. This is not a place
Where cranks can pray upon the native dead.

The day begins starkly, then migrates
From its woodless crypt like a fat termite.
The starry night loses an axle, veers off,
Gets clouded over. Ten moons glow faintly.

O show me the way back into shadows
Of milky galaxies beyond compromise.

My reach limited only by infinity.
Its best pitch can be rightly deduced

Provided existence weighs in the balance.

Twice betrayed! Once with his father's demise,
Second by a witch whose love proved guise.

photo by
david tomaloff

ISSUE NO. 12

a burning flower against
the black sky
climbing toward the atmosphere
its scales purring
whispering

look at me, look at me
I could crush you

and that would be that

— **"Palm star"**
Kevin Ridgeway, page 132

All-Hallows Carnival Villanelle

Jane Røken

It' s just one thing that you may like to know
before our show is done (you' ll beg us stay) —
We take some of you with us when we go.

Come, ride the carousel, and feel the glow
of czardas and a merry roundelay!
Ach, just one thing that you may like to know,

but while the fiddles play, you 'll tip a toe
to other games. Let gold outshine the grey.
We take some of you with us when we go.

Our ghostly band may stanch the seasons' flow
on this night only; then we' re on our way —
it' s just one thing that you may like to know.

The lanterns flicker now; the pipes play low.
As roosters bark and bray at break of day,
we take some of you with us when we go.

So, when the time has come to end the show,
we throw away our jester' s masks and say
one little thing we thought you ought to know:
We take some of you with us when we go.

Unfathomable
Faryn Black

She could already feel the weightless, subtle pull
of her hair floating around her. Unbrushed tangles of seaweed
knotting along her scalp as calliope music blubbered
in waves   —shifting,
        refracting,
                    redacting explanations.

Bare feet had slippyslid
over algae-covered rocks, seabed muck
squishing between toes
as she answered the inexorable
invitation. Spectral jellyfish hovered, swaying
to marine melodies as the beleaguered ceiling of light
surrendered its last distant prism.

Sharks and eels skulking in the deep overhead. She is long past
knowing what form the fins and scales take, brushing past her legs. Cold
on cold is all she knows.
        And the sound.
                    The sound.
                                Further still.

Oblivious to time, unmoved by any current, the ancient beast opens
an opaque eye; her own silhouette a reflected mote in a great black iris.

The shimmyshift of phosphorescence
refuses to illuminate. The unfathomable,
fathoms down. An encompassing perspective
too far back to swim to —she could only point
to negatives. It was not Cthulhu,
nor giant squid. For her, it was not danger.
This cryptid was no stranger.

Ascending in descent: joining the abyssal pantheon
beside her unknowable bridegroom. Damselfish and maids

build her tiara of shells and coral; mandatory attendants
to the lichen-laced forsaken treasure. Welcoming
her reign as thalassic goddess, choirs of aquatic angels
sing her home.

In 1997, an unidentified noise – loud enough to be heard by devices over
5,000 kilometers apart – was recorded underwater off the coast of South
America. Though seemingly biological in nature, any organism large enough to
produce a noise of such volume would have to be many times larger than any
creature ever known to have lived on Earth. Dubbed "The Bloop" by scientists,
the noise was recorded several times over that summer and never heard again.

Dream house
James Dowell

the floor of his bedroom is quicksand.
in the living room a small gnome skitters round
trying to avoid the rays of an electric lite.
in the kitchen sink is a glass and in the glass a
sea.

Mermaid dust

Jean Brasseur

The smell of escape
snakes through words
overflowing the edge of the page.
"Follow the mermaids," they said,
into a Jack the Ripper night.

Rain pelts the window
like a spray of bullets piercing the fog.
Ice tinkles in darkened shadows
and the reader stops to listen
to the rain gathering grief
and sending it down the glass
in tiny streams of indifference.

Was it the weather that imbued
this noiseless relief.
or perhaps it was the scotch?
This question wasted
on a passing windy cloud
before the floor lurched open
and mermaids in spangled
brassieres swam to life,
eyeing him hungrily.

He reached to their glimmering light,
his mouth a round cave
of awe and disbelief.
He had touched a manatee once
but there had been no whisper
of color, no odor of desire,
no reminder of the same loneliness
that followed him everywhere he traveled.

Before his hand pulled
him into the pool, the way out
vanished, leaving behind a trail
of twinkling scales on the polished wood
and armfuls
of empty space.

Family recipe
Jeanie Tomasko

They say I was born in a cold spring, the morning
after my mother put up twelve pints of violet jam.

They say all night it thundered without lightning
and right away I wanted whatever was in the white

pocket of the doctor's coat. They say I was born
with extra layers of seal fat and fine black hairs

on my back. No one knew I would swim
early, swim away before I could even walk.

No one knew you would come with me
through the undulating tendrils of kelp

where we met in a dream and couldn't wake up.
One of your eyes was violet, the other sea-green,

the other I can't say. The complete stories of those
days are inscribed on the rose-colored sand

at the side of the sea. They say it takes five lapfuls
of violets for one jar of jam, a dram of sugar and a spell

said backward. The recipe warns: simmer violets overnight
in white tea. They like to remember the night I was conceived;

they always say: *dew came early on the petals; birds
were singing in the dark. Everything went wrong.*

Valentine on a postcard
KJ

Sorry there was not more on my heart.
Slow is my...my love in filling itself out.
The feelings for you came out yesterday like
a snake leaving a birdhouse one bulge at a time.
Great rolling lengths of warm flesh shaped a shiny
square on each scale for your reflection to quietly occupy.
To have you so close to me laced my blood with endless sugars.
Never mind how starved I am for love, I know that you will be worth
waiting for because I have never opened my heart as wide as you since.

Palm star
Kevin Ridgeway

Shaking for a loose cigarette
the sky clear and the moon full
the southwestern lights illuminating
a distant palm
a star on a Christmas Tree
a beautiful and horrifying vision
of spikes and pricks
with a bleeding gum fanged smile
a burning flower against
the black sky
climbing toward the atmosphere
its scales purring
whispering

look at me, look at me
I could crush you

and that would be that

The devil prowls around like a roaring lion, seeking someone to devour,

Lisa Marie Basile

it says so in the bible, here I am
divining leaves on the bottoms
of bodies and teacups. I want
to know how it feels to be eaten alive.

Glory to God in the highest!
I remember the words tied to my tongue
in a cherry-stem knot. I spit the songs,
plagued, hacking, tuberculosis of faith,
to this day when God has left me for
lions.

I am a naked druid under many moons,
and feel no shame.

My heart condenses desire
like two moths folding into linen,
until I burst.

I am a wet apple-eating machine
and feel no shame.

The hangman appears again,
upside-down. He has a Spanish
face and looks toward the sea.
I envy his ability to understand
things differently, to let those
veins paint his forward.

He wears his mistakes
as the Mediterranean
vast and rough, on his forehead.
I worship only the sea
and feel no shame.

Unholy night
Margaret Mary

My Father,
burned for 200 days, in the Carolinas with his
needle scars and pedophilic psycho angels
begging,
"Star Spangled Banner Save Me"
America — Go fuck yourself with your sadistic statistics
You made me a martyr for illusory Freedom,
Oh Holy Father,
that night you ripped the door handle off
and drove me over broken tarred roads to watch it sail
Into the Land Fill Promised Land.
heroin infected, you smashed my bedroom door
to beg for forgiveness, a patriotic rubber band tied round your bloody arm
and I forgave your sins, Again — your hands burning against
my legs, your blood — pale pink chemical smears that wouldn't
Leave, soaking through my pants
Freedom, I looked for you beneath the cigarette burned sheets that
I buried beneath the house

Holy America, I lied for you

Rituals #1
Melanie Browne

Every night I stay up late,
watching dead Socialites

parade, the snakes crawling out of their eyes,
as the worms play on the sequins in

their Vera Wang dresses,
Ray-bans melting against their skulls,

they fuss and fiddle with their oversized handbags
while gossiping behind rotting silk scarves

voices echo from my television screen
where the living and the dead live it up,

Their quiet and abandoned eyes
beg me to sign their moldy social registers,

I shake my head no, but they force it into my hand where
it crumbles into pieces like their Park Avenue Dreams

Severed body, perfect hair
Rachel Marsom-Richmond

When the
Black Dahlia
was found,
face sliced
into a smile,
her hair
had been
hennaed black,
black
like the clothes
her killer wore,
black
like the darkest moon

Dreaming dogs
Peter Marra

she walked past the chain-link fence:
into the courtyard
she walked quickly
then stopped to
crouch down and listen to the

dog's secret message:
a secret bullet, that's what
the frogs suggested

7 minutes later she lay
on her back on top of
wet moss and dead leaves
and gazed upwards.
underneath, the sidewalk heaved.

she forced the sky from
blue to grey to maroon.
a mutation.
strangled on the monkey bars
dancing in the perimeter

she smiled as she spoke to
the vaginal totems
embedded in the moon
a return to the playground

the thought for the day is:
"exhilaration can kill a biped"

she loosened her corset
allowing herself to breathe as her
black tendrils merged
with the soil.

cremate her soul. she waits for the diorama
and the canine pleasures she can see within:
a feast of victims for a quickening dance with her voice's fury

Come here sweetie

Tess Pfeifle

Come here sweetie, let me caresses you through your dress.
Why do you suppress your want for me?
Why won't you come on over to me?
Your skin so white and pale.
Why are you so cold my dear, why do your eyes seem so far?

Come here sweetie, let me feel your smooth shoulders.
Let me feel the stitches that make you up.
Let me do what I need to do.
You do not make a sound, but you submit so easily.
You get farther every day.

Come here sweetie, are you still resisting me?
I've had you for two weeks now.
I think you've over stayed your welcome.
You've begun to wither and continue to ignore my advances.
You let me caress you.
But you never touch me back.
Why?

Come here sweetie, it's time to put you back where you belong.
I took you back at night, so no one would have to see.
Your walk of shame, you can remain in ambiguity.
I'm sure it's what your family would want.
As I shoveled the same dirt I uplifted two weeks ago.
I think of all the times we shared.
How waking up to you every morning, was what I had always wanted.
Always needed.
And I as I put you back in your coffin.
I kissed you goodnight for the last time.
And I could have sworn.
A tear fell from your eye.

I-5

ISSUE NO. 13

Tomorrow I will feed you the stones from my eyes.
Then while you sleep I'll gut you from gullet to groin
And let your evil loose into the world.
They are my children too after all.

— "Like love"
Lee Gillespie, page 141

The last time
Cynthia Linville

It all starts and ends here:
a stone stairway leading to nowhere.
I recognize the touch of his hand.
Ghosts swarm the skeletal trees.
She is here too,
arms folded back like wings.
A lone broom sweeps the cold path
where we once danced.
An owl hoots thrice:
just one more who betrays you.

* * *

Just one more who betrays you,
she is here too.
An owl hoots thrice.
Ghosts swarm the skeletal trees.
A stone stairway leading to nowhere,
a lone broom sweeps the cold path.
It all starts and ends here
where we once danced,
arms folded back like wings.
I recognize the touch of his hand.

* * *

I recognize the touch of his hand.
Ghosts swarm the skeletal trees,
arms folded back like wings.
She is here too
where we once danced.
An owl hoots thrice.
A lone broom sweeps the cold path,
a stone stairway leading to nowhere.
It all starts and ends here:
just one more who betrays you.

Untitled
Michael Andrew

telephones ringing —
triangles weave
through the dunes

Bite
Harry Calhoun

The seizure makes you strange.
Everyone is not like you, any more
crawling back into the mindless dark

and wakening back to substance
not knowing where you've been,
the green mind you've crawled. The weird mold

of it makes you take medicine as scary and rough
as any terrain you've never crossed, makes you sick and
different and hard to swallow. The spasms

make you strange to yourself, broken ribs
and savage gnawings on your unconsciously bitten tongue
a revenant. A ghost to yourself, words you choose hesitant

and frightening to you as the blood that poured
from you pure, poor lost and ancient tongue.
Chew this thoughtfully and express it as you can

through your vociferously voided self.

Trespasser
John Joe Loftus

A deceased friend arrived with the incoming tide,
departing again before I could awaken
My friend, the tide and me, bound by nothing more than absence

Unidentified
David Russomano

In the years following 9/11, on a brilliant Sunday
morning drive, south toward church down
195, my sister noticed sunlight glinting
off of something hovering over the small city
of Bridgeport. She described it as metallic, but no
aircraft remains stationary quite like that.
Though, in shape and size, it could've been a blimp,
they don't have chrome exteriors or suddenly
take nose dives into city centers like bombs or
rockets. She flinched and braced herself
for an explosion that never came. Later, she
told the story that no one could corroborate.
Life goes on for her, unperturbed by what
she can't explain. But an unbelievable account
from someone you trust is harder to dismiss
than hearsay. I still find the question slinking
around the dim corners of my mind and
occasionally barging forward into the light.

Like love
Lee Gillespie

You kiss me like absinthe spit in the communion cup
And the worm turns and writhes in the blood loamed soil.
The rotten sweet goblin fruit of my womb falls
Into your hand and you bite.

Tomorrow I will feed you the stones from my eyes.
Then while you sleep I'll gut you from gullet to groin
And let your evil loose into the world.
They are my children too after all.

Softly as they leave us
Melissa Bobe

"softly as they leave"   you

beatbeat out
beatbeat out
beatbeatbeatbeatbeatbeat
in   in   in   __
Obscured, she //bound/, was somnambulant in her wooden bed. His
approach, slow(sustained—) up [to the open grave.

And,
Will you join me in a pas de nocturne?
I will.

One grave, one shrouded, one treading, one box. A body//a
body. Two. There are two. There are absolutely two in [this duet;
it is a duet.

But.

(Can you trace the places where the hands graze the sweat and breathing
flesh? Can you find the shadow in the shadow in the empty and abandoned
grave? Can you hear the tap and turn, sinew under suspended skin? If you can,
you are surely watching someone else's *pas de deux*.)

The fifth season
Robert E. Petras

Misty snow dabs pale make-up
upon the brown stubble.
The cattle trough is drained,
the creek bed dry.
Through gauze of white
an island of headstones appears,
gray, flat, canted,
wreathed inside spires of iron.
Steam rises from the fresh, warm soil,
the grave open like a wound,
silent, hollow, seeded,
awaiting the harvest of the fifth season.
A crow caws.

Beating a dead horse
Vivian Bird

Because it was the only thing to me,
I didn't realize it was gone a long time ago.
Even a close friend said, "Think about it."
But I decided not to.
I had thrown out everything I'd owned.
Moved halfway across 6,000 miles.
I'd gotten new friends.
A new job.
Even started drinking vodka
and going by a different name.
But every other good night,
I took my cane out and began beating that beast again.
It wasn't really there anymore, but I still was.
Deep down.
Just me and the wood splitting on the roadside.

Haunted
Richard Cody

Dead men linger 'round your window
most nights
as you lie in bed, sleeping.

Unaware of the dead,
you divide the dark between dreams and oblivion.
You never hear them creeping.

Once, flickering into consciousness,
you mistook a pale face for the moon.

When morning comes they wander
into bar rooms, alleys,
the bushes beside the freeway.

They mingle and hide as best they can,
haunted by your sleeping face
all through the burning day.

Previously published in "This is Not My Heart."

Breaking news (version #1)
Denny E. Marshall

Heard sirens continually blow
Breaking news interrupts the show
Horns sounding not a tornado
First landing of a UFO

Anchor's voice echoing with fear
Stating, the facts are still not clear
Announcement on the radio
First landing of a UFO

Speaking into the microphone
Voice says we are not alone
Reporting a short time ago
First landing of a UFO

The rush of silence
Sam Downum

If I could silence the rush
With more rush
The din of a hundred crashing
Disfigured machines
Consuming each one's bodies
Devoured by the dark light
Of the bastard suns
Those forgotten angels
Spread across the dirt splay
Of man's dwelling (not property)
And wandering with empty
Scarlet eye sockets
To and fro
Of dead childhood memory
Places we were alive
Before we were
One eyed impostors
The black suns forsaken in the
In between – where love
Is course and severe
Flowers with mouths, smiling
And we are whispering
To ourselves

Sleeping like a widow
Sheila Hassell Hughes

She sleeps like a widow, says my mother
who in two years of living alone
has grown fond of the lonely old name
for the way it pins the wings of
her pain so precisely under glass.

She can point to each variation
in shape and shade and coloration and
mark the meaning in the widowed
body of her life, preserved.

She sleeps like a widow, observes
my mother, huddling neatly to her
edge of the bed, mostly empty;
*see how she's clung to the ledge
barely moving, covers unrumpled*

so careful not to disturb the dead
so bold in her flirtation with the long dark line.

That, she says, *is how we widows sleep.*

George Adamski's photo of Venusian spacecraft taken in California (1952), later deemed a hoax.

i want those laughing golden stars.

— **"Ghostly."**
Andrew Chmielowiec, page 148

ISSUE NO. 14

Another creation myth
Catherine Owen

So now I bring you back from ashes,
re-form your small waist, scarred hands, long spine
from dust, take the tiny remnants of finely crushed bone
and re-make your face, its strong jaw, its fragile
way of looking at me and within moments you are
as you were, in one of the rooms we shared, sitting
quite close in a chair, smiling and yes, beautiful,
and I say to you, "What now, that I have brought
you back from the dead?" knowing there is no answer to this,
that your ashes are buried beneath the cedars, unreachable,
that there is no chair and no room, that I have not been able to
start the world over again so I can stop you from dying.

Ghostly.
Andrew Chmielowiec

i want to be the one that
shaking children tell stories about,

on bright nights around
the campfire.

i want them to think that it's

really me

whistling in the wind,
and pulling at their hair.

i want that smell of summer.

i want those laughing golden stars.

To an abandoned cornfield
Chris Kobylinsky

Where the fading trail fizzled out,
Trills of unseen molted crickets
Pulsated in an enclosed field
Covered in prickly cornstalk stubs
And untamed successional growth.
A dome-less silo stood leaning
Slight like an old man ruminating over a chessboard.
Its depressed shadow loomed over
Congruent, parallel furrow-scars;
Its edifice was marred with rust.
Out of its decapitated
Neck, vines had accreted longer
Than Samson's hair. As I took a
Curious step closer, a pair
Of crows, like discovered lovers,
Sprang up and out from behind some
Disorderly, shaggy bramble.

The least musical skeletons
Gus Iversen

There are freshly dead ones
Shaking their skeletons disapprovingly
Like toys from overdeveloped countries
Towards the migraine of eternity

The blunted nuisance of choosing
A chandelier — a sun angle
For noises that install their own
Kinds of sense or something
Undefined and pure in meter

The skeletons that need to be told
When to wake up and go to bed and
Please lay down and be
My xylophone skeletons

Abandoned
Christy Effinger

I remember the day our cars
left town without us.
We came out of the office
at five o'clock
to find them gone.
No note, no goodbye,
just gone.

How many times had they driven us
to work and back again?
How many times had they carried home
groceries and housewares and children?
They took us where we needed to go—
not wanted, but needed to go—
the drugstore, the dry cleaner's,
the bank;
a child's cello lesson or
track meet;
the in-laws' house on Sunday.
Every Sunday.
Every blessed Sunday.

We used to joke
those cars could drive our routes
without us,
but when they finally got the chance,
they didn't.
When they finally got the chance,
those cars drove straight out of town,
away from our state in four different directions.

The cops found Maria's car
1200 miles south on a Florida beach,
tires half-buried in sand,
windows down and doors flung open.
There was pelican poop on the windshield,
an empty rum bottle in the backseat.

Ty's car drove north to Canada,
ran the border and left the road
at the first forest it came to.
It kept going
even when the tires blew out
one by one, even when it was
riding on rims. And when the rims
bent and the axles broke,
well, then it stopped.
Or so the ranger told us.
He told us, too, of the fox
that claimed the car
for her family—call it Karma,
if you consider Ty's record of road kill.

Donnie's car drove itself off a bridge
in Ohio. We should have seen that coming.
It had been sick for years,
dribbling fluid, sputtering at stoplights,
coughing up white smoke
as it rattled around town.
Workmen hauled its rusted carcass
from the river, gave it a proper burial
in a Cleveland junkyard.

My car is still missing.
It was last seen
speeding through Kansas,
headed west across the ripening prairie.
But that was years ago,
and I no longer expect
to hear anything.

For a while after my car left me,
I thought about it
each night when I closed the garage door
before bed, wondering if I should
leave the porch light on
just in case.
And I thought about it again
sometimes between dreams:

why the car fled,
where it was going,
and who would find it
when it got there.

Artemis: Diana, again
Jim Davis

She peeled back petals of the rose
to the core, where our world was.
Now that ephemera been shed, she sings
about a picture of you
bound in a skein of guitar strings –
more specifically, the you that sat at the campfire
on a section of stump taken from the woodshed
at Elmwood Terrace.\\

One day, the absence of familiarity
with a notion like love will fall away, drift to the grass
like petals. Soft, humming sentiment
to which I would
like to identify with
less. Though my cheek bone is swollen
like ripe purple fruit, I design
a map of the far side of this earth's moon – the width of these
United States. Callisto, Ganymede, circle Jupiter
in an orbit that will one day collide, their tragedies
                                    intertwined.\\

Mare Imbrium
Mare Tranquillitatis
Mare Nectaris – where once was water.
And Oceanus Procellarum – the vessel
of one of my weekend poisonings
pouring itself into the pocked face of Diana: ours.\\

Diana, in the early 60s, was a fat, waxing gibbous.
Unlike the waning crescent of this and every day
between 1969 and 1972, when we walked all over her.

Now hear this, you: the practitioners of Santeria
take the head from a Burmese python with a rusted kitchen tool
in praise. Far away, we stab, we enter

that face of moon, pocked and cratered — hung over
the city of my big shoulders, to be congruent

in all our corresponding angles, in pure, Anglo-Saxon text

to be read by false light. The hunt. The violent language of
everything, once it has been, explained.\\

Love smashed us
Michael Dwayne Smith

We spin in our little boy beds. Top speed: imperceptible, inevitable. Waiting
to be split. Collided. Exploding into world. Veering off into our steamy
nights of future. Disappearing, one blue molecule at a time.

Slick-pages under my mattress ignite. Energy, release, repeat—obsession
consumes, an effigy of red licorice. My charred lips will stencil black kisses
over six hundred salty miles of flesh, of curves, and suspense. We shall be
the polluting of sad girls rescued from small town bars, the liquor of one last
hope, fuel burning into gravitational collapse.

Are we still in bed? I can feel the quantum space my organs used to fill.
Oxygen under blankets. I think about good health, the good life, but can't
paint a likeness. And wonder about love, but don't try to hide in anyone's
quiet, or cigarette lit darkness. Green glowing eye of carbon monoxide
alarm, you comfort me more than you could ever know.

Sleep is a paper boat. I'm soggy with memory. Fog creeps over the ocean,
event horizon, and I am, or am not fusion, and I wake or soon imagine I
wave toward a far shore, breaking against an imprint of stars on the rocks
that rock in the sway of cooling planets and tides, floating upside down and
backward, beneath my very own particle-thin slice of inverted yellow moon.

Electric aliens
Lucia Olga Ahrensdorf

with talons of deep pink
and pupils of darting ink
they leapt around the moon

with leopard skin of plastic
and nails of such elastic
they punched a hole into the moon

with yells of screeching clams
and ferocity of sherpan rams
they began to attack the moon

with a sudden hush of painted awe
they all stood silent and hushedly saw
liquid spurt out of the moon

with the viscosity of frozen tea
the rainbow sludge flew gleefully
at the spectators surrounding the moon

they came out of their trance
and began their tarantella dance
happily drinking the juice of the moon

but alas by the rays of the morn
when the sun the color of corn,
shone on the face of the moon

on the ground, there were small holes everywhere
large, dirty, pockmarks, permanently flared
and there was no one to be seen on the moon

Girls with antlers
Richard Peabody

You're not accustomed to girls with antlers
shining whitely from their brows
but you have to admit it turns you on.

"Where have you been?" they chorus.
"They're totally in."

Girls with antlers
carry you from dawn to dusk.

They inflate the bellows.
Massage your neighborhood.

After the ether ponies have raced
around your sarcophagus,

after you've drunk enough potcheen
to attain Celtic blood,

after you've listened to "Danny Boy"
for the 10,000th time,

only then will girls with antlers
anoint your feet with margarine,

steep you in black tea
to dye your skin with tannins,

tie a raven to your wrist
so you may dance

nimbly across moonlit teacups.

If only you could
touch those deciduous horns
stroke that spongy velvet.

Grief season
Meredith Weiers

Turkey vultures hunch
in pines, annual shadows

on the year's X-ray. We
exhume bone china, gift

the porcelain hand
bell a clapper tongue.

On the lace-veiled
table, a rice grain fidgets

in its salt-shaker vault.

Everything's the devil
Ricky Davis

For instance, when you start a car, you put the devil into the devil and turn it.
Then you put your foot on the devil and shift devils, and you drive the devil
down the devil until you reach wherever it is you're going. When you brush your
teeth, you're actually brushing (more or less) 32 devils, using a long devil with
a bunch of little fibrous devils on one end. When you inhale, you're breathing
the devil into your body, which is also the devil. Descartes said that there's
a devil trying to deceive us at every turn, but I don't buy that, since we're all
devils too and that puts us on the same side. Babies are the devil. Old people
are the devil. Dogs and cats are the devil. The earth and the sky are the devil.
So are plants. And birds. Hell, that thing some people call God is the devil. The
devil is the devil. Everything's the devil. But that's okay. Because if everything's
the devil, then everything is exactly what the devil is. And that's everything. So,
everything's everything. Relax.

Things oral
William C. Blome

What a lovely songster is the English sparrow
about his rainspout home; I took to yelling
I'm only divorced five hours since lunch;
the greengrocer's shrill whistle got my attention
yesterday, he sold me some terrific endive;
and my largest pinto pony, hands higher
than any ever on our farm save one, swallowed
pinking shears last Wednesday in his stall.

In Indonesian, ceiling translates as sky sky
Tess Joyce

With such a name,
I often wondered if heaven was a ceiling
where mosquito ghosts would go

to ponder their purpose, to wonder
or panic
that nothing is there but a great bulb of light when we die.

Only nature is present. "Only nature is present"
scares us. Then a thumping. She claims footsteps. I
claim heartbeats.

— "The country at night"
C.M. Humphries, page 159

"Divination"
Helen Vitoria

ISSUE NO. 15

The unpredicted
Anne Butler

In the brown-walled den,
fingers on the pale triangle,
we asked our questions.

The answers were never clear,
but sometimes the spirits spoke:

rattle of windowpanes,
flicker of a street lamp,
a hushed, certain tap.

We held our breaths for initials
of ethereal husbands.

Now I lie with a warm possibility,
Ouija pronouncements hovering
in the future they skated to,
and I start to remember them all—
It's strange what love levitates.

In felt-footed dark, my unpredicted
spells out a past the board didn't know:

First love with The Farm Girl,
soft hulk of regret; fish that ate
each other one afternoon in the tank.

I conjure the tabby cat, dead
of kidney failure while I sang
in the children's choir, his meow
hazy as the tenor line.

And then it materializes
in the feline glow of midnight—

The glint in his yellow-brown eyes
as he pawed the blue house
to the peak of the roof.

Stolen heart
Nicole Taylor

In December, he stole
her heart.

In July, over a year later,
she took it back.

He stole for sport:
bicycles, baseball cards, stereos, music....

He pilfered from
dumpsters, city dumps, and his work.

All privileges were stolen —
trusts, time, rights, dignities.

He burgled hearts, their songs,
and more.

The country at night
C.M. Humphries

Above a thousand fireflies twitter, their glow like shimmering yellow citrines. The bugs become flames. Stalks of corn resemble citronella torches, flames swaying in the wind. We don't intend on turning back to extinguish the flames; don't have the time. We don't care, her and I. Excluding the rush of the wind and the crackling of burning husks, the fields are silent. Only nature is present. *Only nature is present* scares us. Then a thumping. She claims footsteps. I claim heartbeats. Moonlight blinds us, like truck high beams on a country road. Glancing back, I find the light bouncing back towards my eyes from something straight. Something sharp. Something drawing closer. "Please don't let it get us," she whispers, but her voice is too faint for me to hear, for my legs lift me away, like a soul exiting a body. Stalks bend as I dash. She's bumped to the ground. Part of me leaves her there. Part of me returns.

Australian horoscope
Ali Znaidi

The Magpie, March 21-April 20
The sun will return and engulf your realm with sublime lights. You have to seize
the opportunity and capture the cherry blossom before the return of the owl. The
sun will make you amaze people with enigma and light.

The Kookaburras, April 21-May 21
The leaves of the tree woman begin to fall. That is a bad omen. But if you are
brave enough, you can bring luck through chasing the sunrise in Antarctica.

The Bowerbird, May 22-June 21
You can't imagine how mysterious your life would be if you dwell in the cave
for a period of time just to ponder. And if you like to cast a spell on the opposite
sex, just forget about decorating your bower because simplicity has its enigma,
too.

The Rainbow Lorikeet, June 22-July 22
Just keep looking at the horizons because your luck is buried in a little cloud that
is hiding behind the rainbow. The day you will shoot that cloud with your arrow,
the rain will fall and fill in your empty buckets with water of luck.

The Kangaroo, July 23-August 23
Your heart is telling you to stand just in the middle and watch. But your fate
is going to be hit by a beefy brawny buffalo if you don't move. If you find it
difficult to move, just begin with trivial things. Try to change your pillow. Maybe,
a new pillow can make your life start afresh.

The Rabbit, August 24-September 22
Don't drink water all day not just to experience thirst, but also to remember that
your life is inundated with water. So if you like your life to be always fertile just
don't deny the water and grow a rose in the desert to poison any daring snake.

The Koala, September 23-October 23
The crow is coming again cawing to encumber your weary soul. So just follow
that flock of sparrows and listen to their songs— a panacea for all your aches.
Music will fill your termite-infested room with fresh air.

The Emu, October 24- November 22
Never lock your horse in the stable. Just saddle it and start out trying to surpass
the howling wind. When rekindled, your innate power can grow olive trees in
the North Pole.

The Crocodile, November 23-December 21
If you start eating a pizza, just finish it all. Nothing can infest your life but
those crocodile tears. Don't play the role of the victim. You shall overcome all
obstacles, if you don't throw half of your pizza in the dustbin.

The Turtle, December 22-January 20
Some people with prosthetic limbs did cage the dragon. So just uncage fear
from your heart, and don't forget that Venus is watching over you on top of your
shell.

The Eucalyptus, January 21-February 18
Welcome to the wilderness! Finally, you are going to learn how to sleep without
blankets next to thousands of scorpions.

The Redback Spider, February 19-March 20
If you don't know the goat's monologues in the haunted cave, you are missing
out like a crazy. What you need is some strangeness to spice up the emptiness
of your life.

Girl on the highway
D.S. Jones

she went missing midsummer.

she was last seen,
alive out by the highway
and with no clothes on.

when the police came she was gone,
like a squirrel on a tin roof at dawn.

a ghost.
a memory.
someone's little girl, lost.

then when she was forgotten,
by all but her mother, who carried
her picture always, she was found;
by boys who were not looking,
as the gold is often found,
in the ground-by dumb luck.

in a cabin,
in deep woods,
she was
decaying.

Ghost's reflection
Linda Crate

the sun mocks in golden laughter
girls trip over their syllables, skeletons
of their youth spilling riddles of time
against them they just can't see it
yet; soon the light of yesteryear will
stretch ominously longer than they
remember; the ghastly apparition
in the mirror only their childhood ghost.

Natalie
Amber Decker

On his lips

the back and forth of darkening vowels

sets my thighs dripping like slow jazz

He buys me a second drink and I can feel my lips

unfastening like a black corset

Newspaper says the last girl

was strangled with her own scarf

and put out with the garbage

like a botched abortion

It has been 200 days since my hands have touched

another living thing

The grainy image on a security camera

tells my future better than tarot or tea leaves

His hands on my throat an electric shock

the color of rubies

Witch wind
John Grey

"That is no breeze," the young girl says,

"It's a witch's breath exhaling.

And better that you stay indoors,

Before it starts to wailing

And ripping branches free

Of trees, and snapping

Wildflowers at the stem

And with incessant rapping

At your door, begging you open,

So as to sweep you in her flow.

Better a knife blade in the heart,

Than be a witch's beau."

I thank her for her warning then,

Say I will stay indoors,

Not open up to anything,

No witch will get her claws

In me this restless windy night,

Her black arts wont prevail,

I'll be no old hag's fancy man,

No broom's sad human sail.

Eventually the wind dies down

Or blows to distant climes,

And midnight passes, says the clock,

With chilling chortling chimes.

It's time for me to prowl the streets,

Seek out a virgin's blood,

Suck clear the veins of life and love

Then chew my crimson cud.

1 seek no throats of harridans,

No banquet of an age

That scars this flying devilry,

That will not sate my rage.

Better that girl from before,

The one gave me the warning,

I'll thank her for her good advice,

Ami maybe, some sweet morning

When I lie in my coffin bed,

And she dwells in another,

I'll tell her winds may come and go,

But death's a faithful lover.

Possessing what possesses me
Michael Kriesel

"My spirit in the bear knows both
ends of the spear," a shaman chants.
Catullus waits behind him, toga floating.
Open mic night livens up the afterlife.
A Goth girl's punch line bounces
off a Ouija board, finding a woman
possessed by vacationing demons.
"Just another day at the fun factory!"
she hisses at the nurses in Tagalog.
Not her, though it's her tongue.
Same way a leaf lands on my brain
and phrases flood me. Li Po moans,
"So many poems, but no moon."

The lime-green smear
Daniel M. Shapiro

At the side of the freeway
trembling, staring at his shoes,
the truck driver tells
the police officer his story,
a story about having to deliver
500 gallons of paint from El Paso
to Phoenix, how even though the lock
always slipped apart, nothing had ever
fallen out the back, how he didn't even know
it was possible for a paint can
traveling at 70 miles per hour
to crash through a windshield,
hit somebody in the head
and only knock him unconscious
for a few minutes, how he was sorry
about the unsightly mess of lime green
but how lime green beats blood red any day.

Later, light-years above the freeway
chuckling, doubling over,
a space alien will tell
a few buddies his story,
a story about traveling far to assume
the form of a human between El Paso
and Phoenix, how he collided
with a car, briefly transforming
from solid to liquid, how he didn't even know
it was possible for a hyper-intelligent being
traveling faster than the speed of light
to infiltrate the human race so shoddily,
have to pretend to be a miraculously saved man
and answer the questions of a fool in blue
for a few minutes, how he erased the memories
of all including the truck driver, whose green paint
played into the dullness of Occam's razor.

The double
Seth Jani

I am convinced I have a double
Out there, in the blizzards of darkness,
The blossoming nights of May.
A more romantic twin
Courting the stars on their millennial journeys,
Robbing the gardens
Of their fairest rose.

And he is touched by a sweetness
I have only dreamed exists,
And he knows a sorrow
From deep, deep down.

He carries a hundred different crosses
On his muscular back.
He writes poems bird-like and pure.

And when I see in the mirror
My half-witted, bearded face
I understand I am the other one.
The angry attic-ridden brother
Eating sawdust in dimmed-down corners,
Monstrous and alone.

Clarification
Alicia A. Curtis

When she left the wolf,
She came out cawing, all teeth,
His belly a cave.

The woodsman refused
Her the axe. On the mantle
Still: dark fur, pale bone.

A murder, tell the
Child, names any group of crows.
Even old mothers.

Haunted still
Sharon Lask Munson

On an isolated stretch
near Cooper Landing,
five miles past a gravel turnoff,
a simple two room cabin stands.

In that secluded home
with autumn's chill
and darkness coming early,
parents peek in on two sleeping children,
close the door,
drive ten miles to a favorite cafe
for a Miller Light, grilled burgers,
a little conversation —
come home to empty beds.

Search parties comb the wilds —
dark spruce forests,
the confluence of the Kenai and Moose Rivers,
campgrounds battened down for the season.
They peer into boats pulled up to shore,
knock on solitary doors, follow side roads.

It's been thirty-five years since the boy and girl
left their remote cabin —
maybe a trip to the outhouse,
an impulsive evening trek at dusk
in search of salmonberries,
abducted by strangers,
devoured by a grizzly.

Thirty-five years since the story
was plastered on the front page
of the Anchorage Times,
their disappearance wrestled with on local news.

Did they know fear, surprise, cold?
Or did they simply curl up in the underbrush
like wild things, off course, but unafraid
to wait for rescue?

case no. 40619, log no. US-
07082012-0035

ISSUE NO. 16

*— you wake up to the kiss of a machine in the core of
an ambulance, you wake up to the sounds of sirens
and grief —*

**— "On discovering your father's new wife
is an evil stepmother"**
Lisa M. Litrenta, page 175

Subject: flying saucers, information concerning
Emory Bell

"Circular in shape with raised centers
Approximately 50 feet in diameter"
Like lightning drawn to lightning rod
Errant in their tribal, Platonic descent
"It is believed the radar interferes
With the controlling mechanism [sic]"
A trinity of craft, of corpse, thrice
Found in desert Roswell's isotopic sand
"Each one was occupied by three bodies
of human shape but only 3 feet tall"
Some ragged virtue flickers on the
torn edge of an antique sci-fi film,
"Dressed in metallic cloth
Of a very fine texture"
Nuclear Alamogordo, Oak Ridge to Los Alamos;
Now Roswell: center of the conspiracy
"That three so-called flying saucers
Had been recovered in New Mexico"
Home of 25,000 Anasazi sites:
Ancient civilization, atomic detonation, and then
"DATE: MARCH 22, 1950
FROM: GUY HOTTEL, SAC"
Released, finally, by the FBI—
You want to believe? Well Mulder,
this shit is real.

Adapted from a 1950 memo made public by the FBI last year.
It can be found at vault.fbi.gov/hottel_guy

Trophies
Robert E. Petras

See how the crow hops across the spired field
dragging its shadow,
how the skulls blanch,
that the sun does not return the dead.
See how they rest, mounted upon pikes—
all the trophies.
Listen to the bald wind,
how it swoops across the field,
moaning through hollow eyes,
wailing the dirge of a vanquished race.
See the gray dust fleeing like ghosts.
Regard the withered tree,
how the vultures roost, bloated,
patient sentries awaiting another carrion feast.
Your sun turns red.
Tomorrow more trophies shall grace the field.
Tomorrow your skull shall join them.

Untitled
Anastasia Chew

my mistake, i brought the soul in my sweaters
a few spirits and he was courteous enough
to free me of my trappings. we discussed the tastelessness of gin
splashing our intangible abdomens,
how there is not much to do in death
and life but howl at the heavens, and the chore
of levitating pianos. he animated my wellingtons for kicks
and we admired my body wrapped in warm sheets.
soon amassed a littered mob of specters, and they haggled
over myself, cursing each other like witches on a pyre,
covetous of my fingerprints. "Don't," i pleaded but their wan
figures snaked up my ankles and lashed at my chest
"Are you sure?" said pallid Tantalus, "Hysteria suits you."

The voodoo of reverse
Kara Synhorst

I rake my fingers through my hair,
pull out long strands with the tangles,
let them sail out on the wind,
my left hand splayed out the driver's side window.

Despite comparisons
to gold
and cornsilk
the hairs drop and blend, camouflaged,
into cobwebs
and dry leaves.

On the block
where you live
I let fly a fist—
ful. Not voodoo,
willing you to come
to me.

More like the reverse.

Like handing you the
secret key to
my control.

Control my key secret.
Me to come to you willing.
Dry leaves and cobwebs into cornsilk and gold.
Put back the tangles and roll up the window.
The voodoo of reverse.

Doppelganger of a dead boy
Theodosia Henney

I almost drop to my knees on the linoleum
of the airport and cry.
I almost reach out
to touch his face.

I imagine his look of surprise and say
"it's just...
you remind me of someone I knew."

But then the boy in yellow
with the coffee skin and curly hair
is gone, and I still stand in the check-in line,
my breath caught like a barbed fish
in my throat, kicking.

Birdcraft
Jeanie Tomasko

Violet's father shoots grackles in the backyard to keep them from taking over the garden. Violet likes to collect the bodies. She sent for a small colony of flesh-eating beetles to clean the bones. Graveyard beetles, she calls them, and she keeps them in the bottom drawer of a dresser in the basement. When the bird skeletons are lily-white she mounts them on folded cardboard. She's memorized the names of all the bones in a bird's body. Summer afternoons she likes to draw in the coloring book of North American Birds she won at the Science Fair. There's a key at the side of each page with recommended colors for realistic—looking birds. But she likes to fill in the blank spaces with bone structure or organs. The bones are neatly labeled and the organs are colored the way she saw them when she watched the beetles cleaning. If she feels like coloring, she has some blood saved in small bottles. It turns into a perfect color that she can use for the reddish-brown parts, like the rufous throat and chin of the cliff swallow, or the rusty breast of the marsh wren. In a small gold box that was her mother's, she saves all of the eyes.

Tender
Morgan Adams

From a distance it resembled a rather large man in a fur coat,
leaning tenderly over the grave of a loved one. *

A bear follows the smell
of bitter meat, breaks open
the casket and eats, uses teeth
to separate fat from bone. Then
it teaches another bear how
to find the softest dirt, fresh-turned
and sweet. Together, they slip
their claws into wood seams
and wrench satin lining free.
Under each headstone, new tastes:
powder and bleach, a stiff ankle,
stitches, and ethanol to help
the flesh keep. The bears feast.

*From opening line of "Russian bears treat graveyards
as 'giant refrigerators'." The Guardian, October 26, 2010.

Darker days
Cheri Anne

80, 90 miles per hour means nothing to me.
Remember tracing my skin with mother's kitchen cutlery,
seeing how much it'd take to fill up the sink.
Had a gun aimed at my face without the instinct to blink.
I've had hands gripped 'round my throat,
and underneath my Sunday school dress.
He took from me and left nothing,
but I have made it through with much less.

Untitled
Kyla Cheung

I have begun to hear something screaming at night. I don't know if others are listening or can hear it even, but I'm not going to say a word. It started a week ago, hours after he left, and it sounded like some girl child. She had probably gotten lost. Probably been mauled when I remember the hoarse yelling. The screams came in regular intervals. The beats were predictable. The terror was portioned out in chilling and orderly servings. My eyes remained closed, and I stayed inside, in my bed, quite certain that it was just an animal I heard. A possum perhaps, but certainly something wretched and nocturnal. Something motherless. Ugly. White-furred.

In the morning, the man asks me if I want some coffee. Would I care for some milk. At night the screams wake me once more. As they do the night next, and the next.

On discovering your father's new wife is an evil stepmother
Lisa M. Litrenta

It makes sense now: your mother died. Your mother died, and your father, he couldn't be alone. He feared for you, too — the motherless child. Secretly, he dreamt of her arms, legendary and silk white. He hid these fantasies, buried them beneath sweet talk for the new woman. He was blinded by grief. You knew. You knew she was evil. His love, the white of your arms, she was jealous instantaneously: she invested in charms to soften the skin, to lighten age spots, to delude herself into thinking he loved her— that it was her name he called in the night. Days dragged, skin wrinkled, and she grew bitter. There are numerous plots. You are sent into the woods with your brother on false pretenses. You escape the witch's house, pockets weighed down with sweets and revenge. You are sent into the woods again, and she bewitches every brook. You leave a queen, your brother transformed from boy to deer to boy (and no, he will never be quite the same again, the way he gazes at the moon,) Once again, the woods. A failed murder. This time, she hides herself in a witch's costume — you snicker that it isn't far off her natural look— she angers, feeds you something with apples — your allergy is legendary — you wake up to the kiss of a machine in the core of an ambulance, you wake up to the sounds of sirens and grief —

Dog thoughts:
Tyler Burdwood

A dog barks, "Wood shed. Wood shed."
The weather has tattoos and my couch
is ragged, whistling, fucked. A chain-link
bench, cold-cutted from the bass drum pig's
upright parade, passes our skunk-game
of murder-in-the-park. The swing sets country
western-cow licks, stifled by God's bear hug.
Sunshine, broken open on a sidewalk,
is not fat but a miracle of buoyancy.
I overcame my can-do attitude.
Burroughs is buried in a dorm room.
My friend kicks cop-shins shouting "Fascist!"
I am nervous. I am trying not to laugh.
Fin wildly like the claw found your jugular.
I bought a prank can of nuts at a yard-sale.
Peel away the lid: God pops out.
The springs are sharp enough to be dangerous.
I am birthday candles.
I am wax-on frosting.
I am ipecac. I am charcoal.
I am clam-baked in the trove
where everyone's virginity is stored.

My dream that we are spirits
Roy Bentley

I had decided to pray. I had been eating buffalo for months
and asking others to do the same. I asked my dead uncle,
in the ground for thirty years by then, whose Olan Mills
portrait in a frame graced the top of a chest-of-drawers,
to intercede in a matter of some importance. He heard
a prayer delivered in the way Catholics pray to saints—
I spoke to that framed image of him I'd kept nearby for
all those years—and the prayer was answered. I forgot
to thank him, thank Whomever, until I was watching
a program on Native Americans. Heard how the buffalo
came up, out of the earth, to feed the people of the Plains.
The beast was named "Majestic One"—with a Sioux word
the pronounciation of which I'd be unworthy to attempt.
Josh Brolin was knocking around, in a History Channel
movie with its wide river panoramas, fighting bears and
having to get someone to stitch his scalp back on, and
I remembered the prayer. And toasted the spirit of Billy
Potter with a good Kentucky bourbon because I knew
the water in the whisky came from where he was born,
where every morning light touches the people as if for
the last time, in Letcher County, a place without buffalo
where words like majestic aren't voiced much. Before
he got God, he'd have estimated Existence as: We fight,
we fuck, we die. Something like that. A thing men say.
Then he joined a sect of Protestantism that calls itself
Holiness. His mother had been Old Regular Baptist.
These sing hymns where lines of song are given out
before being sung without accompaniment or with
the barest of instrumentation. It no longer matters
whether he was right about God being this thing
we carry with us. I have his voice, holy or human,
in wind that practices the art of call-and-answer.

It's hard to have conversations
Hillary Lyon

you take 4 to 6 hits a night
(single-malt scotch,little ice, no water)
I suck on rock salt
tell you I saw Ted Bundy
in the deli section of the grocery store
this morning and he saw me
with those glassy shark eyes
and he stood behind me in the check-out line
reading my name & address off my check so close
I could smell the incense of Old Sparky in his hair —
it is not all that different
from the smell of your cigar

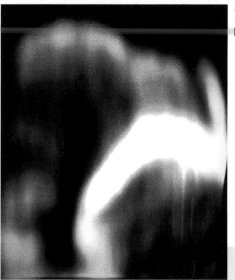

Fertile isn't the right word, but it grows
an arm, or a tooth, leftovers from the night
before. An engagement of knives and forks
sawing through marrow and bone.

— **"There are folds in this television"**
Laura Grodin, page 184

ISSUE NO. 17

Burned alive
Emily Rose Cole

It was just as you might expect:
I blistered; I howled; I leaked
insufficient moisture to extinguish myself.
As the first of my ashes caught the wind,
the arsonist approached the charred ground
and apologized.
As if I were not cinders now.
As if "I'm sorry" could jumpstart a resurrection.

Next time, I will choose not to be born
in a body that breathes, that wants, that needs.
I will cast myself in iron,
melt and mold myself
into swiftest steel,
severing limbs and razing hearts
easy as lying.

Next time, I will not fear the inferno
that rises like a whirling gypsy,
inviting me to her burnished arms:

next time, I will love her,
and she will love me back.

This poem is not about you: a post-break-up spell
Cynthia Linville

Say your beloved's name backwards three times.

Box up every love note, every gift. Seal the box with a double knot.

Smudge every room with wormwood, mugwort, and sage, and sprinkle coarse salt over all the windowsills and doorways.

Stay out all night dancing.

Take a new lover.

Post pictures of the two of you, smiling, all over Facebook.

When someone asks about your ex, look puzzled and say, who?

Flightless bird
Jackson Burgess

Every pair of plastic breasts and 2-D thighs in the world
couldn't make me feel any less alone tonight
as I look out over the city and think maybe falling isn't
so bad, as I do every bone-cold evening here
in L.A.'s central nervous system with head
in hands and teeth crumbling in mouth—you know,
they say when you hit ground zero in dreams
you rise awake and I've killed myself enough times
to know tower-diving has been linked to
post-mortem depression and heartbeats pumping
four-letter-words in Morse code, like "love" and
"care," and "fuck," so pull a couple punches,
go ahead and take in a lungful before
I scrape you out of my throat with all the other
almost-lovers whose tongues fought my teeth and lost.

Reading with Miranda
Eric Roalson

We first met at the Fiction Desk. We were checking out the same book. When I first saw Miranda she was loitering by the Soap Center. I bought some bleach and told her this was the first page.

Thus began our days of gladiolas and lacksadasies. I fell in love with her radiator teeth and jalapeno tongue. They made my dragons sing. I caressed her and the roses breathed. Her palm tree hips rode my wind drum horse. The pages were turning cartwheels of ecstasy, cartwheels of joy.

Miranda had brick windows and x-ray eyes. "A salmon trout leapt out of the venetian blinds into a picture frame pool," she told me. Or was it into the frying pan? I should have takes notes on everything inside of Miranda quotes.

That summer Miranda kept a bat in the refrigerator. One night in July, she had a dream as deep as hibernation. However, when she opened her eyes the next morning, the bat flew into our bedroom. The refrigerator was missing and she couldn't remember the dream. That was a strange paragraph in our lives.

The next chapter brought several dramatic changes. Sure we had to eat a lot of canned goods and fast food burgers, but the worst part was Miranda seemed constantly elsewhere. I couldn't believe what I was reading. She would often be out of town for long periods to attend UFO conventions across the globe. Even when Miranda was at home, she was somewhere else: constantly pouring over maps of the Milky Way, painting nebulae pastels, or watching the George Lucas commentary track for "Star Wars."

I thought we were checking out a romance novel together. What went wrong? Then one day, I read the back of her copy. It turns out she was reading the Science Fiction version. Not only was she reading different content than I but this also meant she was at least one chapter ahead of me. No wonder the wind drum horse had been put out to pasture.

I returned my copy to the Fiction Desk that very night. I had to pay a late fee but it was worth it to end the plot of this sad romance. When I left the library, I saw threatening lights in the heavens. Suddenly, my refrigerator fell out of the sky like a giant exclamation mark onto my head, killing me instantly.

The park
Holly Day

at night
the whistling of the wind
through the leaves of the old maple tree
at the heart of the park
sounds just like a baby
sighing in his sleep

if I was
even slightly superstitious
you might even say the sighing
of the wind through the park at night
sounds just
like the last
dying gasps of

the baby they found abandoned
under the tree
last summer
stroller filled so high
with autumn leaves

Getting lost
Changming Yuan

God says I am a man
Man says I am a ghost
Though I am neither but a spirit
Trying to locate a human shape
Where I can settle down
Like a baby crow flapping
Its young wings against dusk
Hoping to find a spring twig
To perch for the cold night

There are folds in this television
Laura Grodin

Fertile isn't the right word, but it grows
an arm, or a tooth, leftovers from the night
before. An engagement of knives and forks
sawing through marrow and bone.

What's left once you've picked off the meat?

Fragile is the right word, coursing through the vein
like a pin-prick, puncturing a pulsing crevice,
a shadowy stench of tomorrow's morning,
the aftertaste a memory on your throat.

Can night grow from an infant seed?

You can dismiss the rattling of empty
pipes, a letter-box painted hollow
by routine checks, green from a summer
that's long passed, inches in the grass.

Those inches wrap around the skull.

The summer moths come home, tucked
like sprouts in crumbled soil, swung around
the frame, a canopy of parts.
The tendon, the wing, the spoon.

Thought 453
Mora Torres

I watched as her sweater slowly devoured her.
From the moment she discovered the benign-looking thing,
it started insidiously gnawing at her wrists
until it sucked up her thumbs
and finally ingested each finger with a slurp
leaving only the gaping maws of hanging python sleeves
with the telltale lumps of her bony fists
awaiting more complete digestion just inside the cuffs
from which her hands used to hang.

The sweater sucked the fat from her neck and face,
her hood subtly chewing off the ends of her hair—
gnawing her head to total alopecia
before licking out the light from her eyes
like whipped cream off a sundae.

The sweater spread to her bones and her spirit
consuming her femurs until she could no longer stand it
and her cold feet folded easily into the sweater's inviting mouth
her own mouth fading into the draw-string pursed lips of the knitted abyss.

She breathed her last few rattling breaths
before the sweater swallowed those too.

How to manipulate people: a legal slave
Molly Hamilton

Beloved be warned.

Find someone that doesn't' have any friends, a good family, and few belongings. Watch them from afar. Wait for him to go through a crisis. The very young and the very old are great candidates.

You have found someone you can control. This person won't leave you—you will make sure of that! This person will be yours. Hide fear. Approach him. Be confident, authoritative, but kind. Make him run to you. Have him believe he needs you. Guide him; always be with him. Explain everything by your wise standard. Wait for him to make a mistake.

He broke one of your rules of life. He defiled your authority. Do not be scared. This is only the first time. Explain why he was so bad. Tell him how you told him not to stray from your teaching. Make him feel absolutely terrible, but do not punish yet. Right now you are establishing your wisdom.

Watch him, watch him closer. He knows he broke the trust. Give him more instructions, more rules. Award his behavior. Show how beautiful life is when you are obeyed, but bring up his mistake often. Do not let him forget.

He messed up again. Now you are in danger of him rebelling. Now he must be punished. Show the consequence. It is your decision in how you punish: mental or physical. Make him deeply sorry. Pretend you may throw him out even though he needs you. Watch him beg, plea, cry. Forgive him now. Exaggerate the mercy you have for the dirty little rule breaker. He knows only you could love him. Watch him make promises. Make him grateful for your forgiveness.

Be kind again, but punish for now on. Make up again. He won't ever leave.

Finally, having stopped at a diner, i am able to think.
Nathan Lipps

After great pain, a formal feeling comes — Emily Dickinson

I am eager to empty these coffee cups.
I am a car, broken down, near the bluffs of L.A.
I am a god, walking in the nakedness of a mechanic.
I am the breasts that fill the bra of this tired waitress.
I am the scars that flag my back, like dried up riverbeds in a darkened desert.
I am the desert.

And we are sitting here. Tapping our spoons on empty plates. Pinching sugar packets between fingers, the grains lost in our calloused palms. Looking for a fiery accelerant to bang us, rocket-like towards newer celestial neighborhoods. We, the foreigners plopping down next door. They don't want us, they won't have us.

I am the crucifix hanging from the mirror, clashing against the faux pine paneled dashboard.

I am the tender sway of silence, flipping men on their heads, asses to the sky.
I am that bracing moment when all beliefs break away. And I am eager.

The bone man
Neil Weston

Bodies buried in a time of ritual
Settled deep underfoot is
Dug over by the archaeologist
Scraping away the past digging up
Memories.
They said the odd was hounded to death
People liked to say such things if terror was
Resultant.
The archaeologist rarely listened to rumour
He was interested in the bones
Skeletons of those that travelled
This dug up
Road.
Rain lashes the rim
The hole collapses and clouds
Gathered in resplendent
Black
Pay homage to the archaeologist lost digging his
Hole
Lost in the
Mud when the walls
Collapsed
Becoming one with the ancient
Bones.

Very cold day
Jude Cowan

The doctors do not know what ails him.
All is sunshine in the west. Keep him in bed.
Five years ago we had a very windy day.

I'm glad they've left us a few boats. A walk
To the docks will do us the world of good.
Him in his pram, getting pretty close to it.

I haven't got long before the monoplanes.
I bought a straw hat but it doesn't suit me
so I gave it to the donkey, got a great laugh.

The child's coffin is measured by teeth.
One for each day of the week. I fell over
again, just at the spot where it happened.

Aliens
Stephen Bunch

They have been here all along,
not Andromedans or even Mexicans.
They conduct experiments on their
spouses,
abduct their children,
drive the whole family
to Disneyworld on vacation.
They build slab houses and gated estates,
five-star restaurants and liquor stores
with drive-thru windows,
not pyramids or sidereal stelai
or interstellar bridges.
If they were telepathic they'd know
we don't need mind readers, that each
of us is the other, they'd know
their own shadowy thoughts

ISSUE NO. 18

when we can no longer pass for Living, let's disguise
ourselves as ghosts, steal the still warm wedding sheets
veil our pink skins with white linen.

— **"Will-o-whisp"**
Mary Elzabeth Lee, page 197

Murder poem
Kristin Maffei

Every boy I meet could be you, killer.
I've known since age five. I dreamt corpses
hanging from the red maple in the yard.
You put something in the trunk. It was me.

I'll be Janet Leigh and you can wear a wig.
I will be all chocolate syrup creeping
down the drain for you. This is how it goes:
I am showering. "Don't," I scream. Or else

I wake to your breath on my throat. Or you've
been fighting with your mother. You sever
my head, use my mouth like a Real-Girl doll.
They find my fingernails and nothing else.

Your knife presses against my stomach, taut
on the spot where my boyfriend used to come.

Into the storm
Jean Brasseur

calypso, calliope, canopy
the words stick in my head
like elevator sex
and your eyes of glass
I don't want to be a bitch
but I wish
you would all leave me alone
to drive fast
into the fog
Unforgiven playing loud
to wet pavement

until the dirty teeth of night
pierce my thoughts
and devour them
like tiny rabbits
spit out the soft fur
these few lines
and the crystal stars
of your eyes

Postmortem cohabitation
Francis X. Altomare

Sharing a bathroom with your dead fiancée
is never easy, especially with her
shaving cream and razor still sunbathing
on the mildewed shower sill,
rusting late into the Florida afternoons.

Plus, she paces through all the mirrors relentless,
wearing that diaphanous summer dress, you know, the one
you loved best, the one you buried her in beneath
the dunes; and she's always asking the same silly question,
holding up two silver hoops: does this match?

At dusk, more traces: her eyes, whistling
sawgrass, hair like braided bran,
her laugh a champagne cork,
and perfect alabaster teeth
suspended midair.

You quiver as she broods in the corner
still trying to decide what to wear
even though her wardrobe is scattered
across Goodwills in five counties and none
of the precious scraps you've kept complement her stilettos.

How long do these echoes last? It's been one month
since the world ended for you both,
the hottest day on record (the bees are still gossiping
about it along the brittle grass) and though she tries
she cannot drink from the tap
which spouts only cheap wine and unfortunate rumors
such as these.

Wild magic

Laura LeHew

We were hot pants,
hip huggers, purple velvet
"Smoke on the Water and Fire in the Sky"

We were truants changing into jeans and cropped t-shirts
in the copse of dogwoods in Mort Jacobs Park
slathering on Coppertone making our way

thumbs out to Northwest Plaza in the heat in the humidity
to splash in fountains push strange boys to the brink
their scent Gandalf and Aragorn and Ent

We were junior high, we could have said no:
babies, drinking, drugs; we could have all gone on to high school,
our counselors advising us on colleges, SATs,

student loans, someone somewhere could have
commented, shown us a way out of our bruises,
broken psyches, bad choices

Instead of light grey Mourning Doves our soft calls laments
we could have all become Fire-tufted Barbets our striking
plumage green with bits of red, blue and yellow

our voices the spirited song of cicadas

Off the sill
M. J. Luppa

Walking out into the night
and November rain, the windows
on Admiral Park are dark, except one
with its steamy blue light on—

There's a thin man caught
behind the shade. He leans back
and forth— you can feel
his scrubbing with soap and rag—
see his leaving, the ghost
dripping

For lack of an open window high above the lane
Michael H. Brownstein

She came home with a present of matching mopeds—
What an interesting way for me to commit suicide, he said,
And once when she posted their photograph on his page,
She tagged it: He's creepy, but I'm the cutie.
She had this way of weaving stretch marks across his brow.
At night after the music is put away, after the dinner plates
Are piled into the sink, after the pots are left to soak,
They lay in bed together, she reading the full account
Of Mandelstrom throwing himself away because he had to.
She does not know he has already recorded it,
It and the words aura, animosity, abyss, anthrax.
When she curls away from him because she has to, he kisses
The back of her neck, pulls his hands to himself
And whispers, "Sweet dreams, my Nadezhda,"
Every activity, every encounter another attempt at suicide.

The Mad Hatter
Jeannine Geise

I have spoken often of his eyes. Gravel-blind,
he forced blood in his eyes, muttering
prophecy: ostrich, toothpaste, Turkish,
toast and teakettles. Flapdoodle! We're all mad here.
My body is a cabinet full of caterpillars. Leaves
are sprouting in my hair, buds blooming
through my eyes and throat. Haloed, I am hidden.
Each step feels like its own miracle, but white
eludes us like time, a melted pocket watch. He was
vulnerose, tuberose, many bone flowers shining
in the moonlight, metacarpals shimmer. Death
he saw as always being beautiful, love like
a burning tire under the cracked, grey sky.
As a child he was given a wounded bat, spirited
it away to his hiding places. Next morning, it lay
half dead, covered with frenzied ants. Overcome,
he bit into the writhing mass, decapitation
the highest honor. I always enjoy
when the dead talk.

You are really scared
Cindy Rinne

infrared ash exhumed
supernatural beings crash
in the clouds when will
I get water tea-stained
tusks crushed to dust a leaf
zigzags grasping aerial
sea taps as it touches
stone the spirit of the tree
speaks you seek to leave
star beings behind

Roswell observatory
Michael Keenan

After searching
out some castle off the Carolina

     coast,

and finding it,

and finding that the world, after

     all, isn't as small as a turquoise

          army winking

at Lon Chaney as the wolf
bane blooms

for the very last time, in
love, or at

the very least, on fire.

After all this,
we come home to

Alcatraz

to find the old house up for sale,

          and the right-hand-man

     to the stars already forgetting

our secret names. Hiroshima, we come home

to Alcatraz, and Emily sleeps, David
too exhausted to save her

tonight, and the world asleep, and the world the same, when

something stirs in the dark.

Will-o-whisp
Mary Elzabeth Lee

when we can no longer pass
for Living, let's disguise ourselves
as ghosts, steal the still warm

wedding sheets veil our pink skins
with white linen. ignore the floral
print, the wayward threads.

let people wonder
at the wisps and cusps of our
whispered conversations;

swear
avenge me
swear.

let's lead children astray
down wishing wells, wail
with widows on Wednesdays, cross those

burnt bridges to the attics of our once
well-meaning friends. make our way
to their torch-lit porches, wave at them

the words of Aaron, with one quick
edit: Let not your sorrow die, though
I am not dead.

Despot, lust and sorrow
Marina Rubin

But what I really want is a hat
with enormous black brims
so I can walk in the city of phantoms
and hit everyone on the shoulder
or in the face, depending on height

Mojave ghost story
Michael Dwayne Smith

How often I've heard it whistling through canyons.
A name, like a cowboy lost among dead stars.
I know the apparition I'm supposed to see in this:
ghost rider, violet silhouette in a pale desert moon.
I get a feeling that spills out of the clouds, like
mourner's breath, but a little less air, a lot more Zen.
Men die in thin atmosphere. Squint into cottonwood
strung with corpses like shirts on a line. Squat
on the edge of the Great Cliff. Before looking down,
a glance over the shoulder at the wide plain, continent
of femur and skull and useless blood. Little rivers
running backward in time, boatloads of confused eyes
searching for clay on the banks, for shape, for home
in a country of midnight. Every one of them claims to
feel a hand hover above—reaching for a soul or for
a holster, none can say. The ghost rider turns away
to peer down, down deep into coyote's eye. Angels
and wings don't mean much out here. It's cool water,
dry boots, the musculature of backs and the guitar of
a woman's body, music wading up from matted fur
into fire, ash strumming into thin atmosphere
where the slight light of early dawn wets the wick
of one dead star at a time. Ghosts go to bed alone,
palms cradling a language never spoken,
scrambling up dream ladders to a dry lake moon
where love is lost in the desert of white, and a violet
cowboy falls like a Buddha on the peak of his knife.

Night breaks
Molly Kat

my fingers lose feeling
as I stare at the white
glow and wish I were
Bukowski

wish I could write to you
in night, in dark ink
on a napkin smudged
with lipstick

play out a future
of Hollywood and pipe dream
or nightmare
pipe bomb
accidental pregnancy
black eye, broken heart
listening to you piss
in the bathroom
curse your name

it's best
you hitchhike south
I drive north
fall in love
with the slow drawl
of your words
never curse you
hate the day
you came bloodied into
the world

screaming

but I am not Bukowski
and I'd rather know
for sure
the no in my throat
then guess

be suspended in maybe

I dream in black and white
lately, and reflections appear
where they do not belong
but I saw color in you
that daunting cold blue
dark and bright at once
the need to hold it
again, shake it loose
anaconda myself around you
or you around me

we'll take all the books
to bed with us

grow limbs made of paper
strike a match
and burn burn burn

until night breaks
and falls from the sky.

"Fairies" captured by profressor John Hyatt

ISSUE NO. 19

Ruinous silence
salts her eyes: beautiful dogs,
gone the way of the swans –
where are the missing dead?

— "Berlin, 1944"
Steve Isaak, page 208

Freaks
Israel Wasserstein

Stare at us: twins, bound by flesh and chance;
a woman with a beard so full, so immaculate
you wish it is yours; a man whose
flesh is remade in ink and iron.

Each of us shaped by birth or choice,
until you stand frozen before us like possums
crowding night roads, dreaming yourself unique
among the faceless throng.

You think us radically individual, we who survive
by being unlike you. But we are one,
shaped in taunts and whispers, forged
by seizing what you call weakness.

You believed us alone, lawless, without recourse,
discarded as rags, bones behind the carnival.
Now, the price. On four legs, or two, or none, we surround you.
So used to leering, yet you overlook us, until

we take hold. Come: we will reshape you.

Hum of the spin
Denny E. Marshall

Could see soft lights hear the hum of the spin
As the UFO is gently landing
Could not make out details from the cabin
Could see soft lights hear the hum of the spin
From hatch, emerge forms of strange origin
Other ships land their numbers expanding
Could see soft lights hear the hum of the spin
As the UFO is gently landing

Bildungsroman
Alex Ehrhardt

you ask the wise woman
how it is you will know
what to do with yourself.

she gives you a recipe.

put in your pan cayenne, honey, and a little pig's blood.
leave it to burn

you do. At first, it smells
like itself. Like three things
together. Then just carbon.

You bring it to her to ask
what do I do with this
and her forest is burnt

toothpicks laid in a row
and the ashes of stones.
the wind blows through.

there's something in your eye. you tear
it's still there. you gush and gush nose
and eyes and throat and pores.

you are the wettest thing in this dead
place. the ashes are mud now. your boots
are wet. you cry and snot yourself a bath

the mud was ash and tears
the ash was rock and house
and deer and child and it is all on you

it presses every bit of your skin
you know the place of every bit of your skin
you slough it off. leave it to soak.

you bleed back to your house.

you make yourself a bed of gauze.
lay down with your frypan.
cook the bloody scraps that fell in overnight.
this is your breakfast. this is how
you will start your days from now on.

Tardy postcard
Ricky Garni

When they demolish your house,
I want to be there.
When they treat you for death,
I want to hear that you feel great.
When that guy beans you with a baseball,
I want to be able to say: Go Get 'Im, Tiger.
When you forget who you are,
I want to follow you from the hospital
to the shelter.
I will be the one
with the balloon
that is red and fat
and no one knows
is really a satellite
for watching you.
I want to join you on another
earth that looks just like this one,
only smaller, and live
in a beautiful house—the size,
the feel, of a warm, kind toaster.

Rocks
M. Krochmalnik Grabois

I'm coming apart like a meteor
entering Earth's atmosphere

My top hat flies off my head
and bursts into flame
but only for a moment
not even a moment

The moon is my heart
full and blank
The craters have been erased

All these rocks that used to be my shoulders
now they're just rocks

Diagram of daughter
Jacob Luplow

Moments before the dreams began,
I'd hear the moths clink around in the walls
like bits of glass:

I had been there once already to remove
the rats from the crawlspace
and now the rats have wings
and their stories are different—
from scratching to clinking to
sounds dispersing through reeds and falling slow
to stones of onyx and charcoal red
smooth
fresh from the tumbler:

how I see it in the thin moment
between wake and sleep.

In 1988, my daughter skinned the family cat.
We sent her to a mental ward where
she watches mercury travel darkness—
like lotus through glass, pulling blood along.

In a letter once, she wrote:

In a glass box there you are on your hands and knees
watching the paint peel back from the walls,
the drawings they hold from a child's
strangered longhand, all peeling back in flakes
of asbestos and lead based colors.

You like it that way, daddy. The toxicity.

You look through the bare glass, can hear my steps
light and thin and stretched real long.
They come in increments and slow to disembody—
sounds of fire ants charged with cocaine.

And there I am, a flamenco dancer dancing in fog.

I creep with narrow strides. Fog the glass
with my breath and my finger passes right through.

But daddy, you must know, when I get out,
I will siphon you—

pulling a collapsed silk web from water.

Elevator down
Taylor Graham

Step inside.
Look at all the bored stressed—
out blank faces.
Launch into Gregorian chant.
Tell them you've never gotten over
your fear of heights.
Ask if this elevator might
be hijacked.
Repeat Schnellzugzuschlag
quickly ten times.
Ask how fast an elevator
falls
if the cable breaks.
Ask about the center
of the
earth,
and might the elevator plunge
that far.
Offer to read your own
personal elevator poems.
Ask if you'll see
the bones of miners
on the way down.
Another poem of your
own, as many as it takes
to reach your floor.

Feed the lake
Denise Rodriguez

for Jake

*"All that matters is feeding the lake. I don't matter. The lake matters. You must
keep feeding the lake."—Jean Rhys*

You lie on your stomach
your arms folded underneath
your body— a wild gypsy drunk off wine.

There are devils in the cards,
chained and waiting.
The moon inside our chests bleeds
a lake of light and cold dust.
Feed the lake.

> *Temperance—
> masculine and feminine
> are one universe.*

> *All the knowledge that exists,
> exists inside our bodies.*

We search for a key
to the door to make the door
open.

> *Feed the lake,
> make the door open.*

Mondays
Margaret Mary

I will break you,
you have a deer's heart
it
slams between your
        thighs
&
        you have the eyes of a vulture —
you push them along my stomach
concave, I will bury my face —
you're too cold for
the pupupushing
        of your neck into my hip
digging your fingers into m—

Zebras in purgatory
Monica Rico

There is a wait and you don't show up.
Never appear in dreams as promised.
There is no other side. Nothing
happens, you said, nothing.

I think of you when a crow caws,
a voice that reminded you steadily of Robert
Plant.
And I remember your zebras
because what would be the point in riding a
horse through purgatory.
The zebra looks cooler, you said and all the little
girls would be jealous.

Berlin, 1944
Steve Isaak

Crumbling city:
flesh-taut skeletons shuffle silently
past niveous lake,
vain swans now
sullied bones on cracked plates.

Ruinous silence
salts her eyes: beautiful dogs,
gone the way of the swans –
where are the missing dead?

They reside
in his eyes: his lupine touches
tamed, sullied by war, doubt;
equally devoured, she freezes.

The wolves
Joe Nicholas

talk to the moon because they're lonely,
even together,
but the moon doesn't listen,
and has her back
turned to them,
and her cratered eyes fixed
upon the bowels
of space filling
with radiation
bubbles, and burning
coffins,

and the wolves
keep talking,
and feel a little less
alone,

even though
they aren't.

With each handful you dead
Simon Perchik

With each handful you dead
breathe in, nourished by dirt
by these leaves half stone

half come to a stop —without a breeze
your mouth smells from some quarry
that has no past —you are fed

among flowers and slowly behind
go on eating, adored, immense
seething with mountains

no longer outside, creaking
or far away another bedside
fragrant with lips and whispers.

Yellow bone among the stars—
a vision, like a saint—
pull your memories up by the eye sockets
and you shall,
with time,
be pretty yet.

— "Yellow bone"
Catherine Cimillo Cavallone, page 217

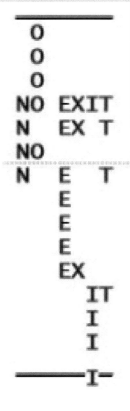

"No Exit"
Jim Eigo

I planted my garden
Joan McNerney

on the wrong side
of the moon forgetting
tides of ocean
lunar wax wane

only madness
was cultivated
there underground
tubular roots
corpulent veins

flowers called
despair gave off
a single fruit...

I ate it
my laughter
becoming harsh
my eyes grew
oblique.

The ancient map
Joe Love

From Babylonia we rode
the skeleton of a camel East

you wanted to ride shotgun
so the cleric drew a basket

from snakeskin he found
by the light of the new moon

*if it isn't a new moon
you don't want it*, he said

and we believed him and opened
up the parchment tied with

a palm branch taken from the last
tree standing on the entire planet

it was our map
and it told us we would journey

until we reached the end
and the cleric laughed

and said *it lies*

Disappeared
Cassandra de Alba

Unkept lighthouses blink electric
at lobster boats, boards on beach house
windows, the stiff crash of wave on cliff

The girls under the dunes
beat their palms against the sand

The beach pulses with them
if you've got the right eyes

January is the best time to look:
the restless cold
the pound of the ocean

like a pretty mouth
chewing on police reports
like a mother's heartbeat
pulling them home

Preterist
Joseph Harms

This glacis where is leavened frore by frore
and beauty memento mori; to wake
and dream of sleep from adamantine noon
to keloid vesp when not at abattoir
(these factories like life fulfill clichés);
the killall's ken; the procinct's penury;
the manse so seen beyond the rye approached
but never entered./ Noses nuchal neath
her porch by spiders traipsed to Az said Bel,
Just stop. Be still. Be still. We're lucky to
feel them. One day I'll smell of ozone; you
too thin to matter. Ghosts with blood. No one
will ever touch us. No. Except for blood.
So few but us don't want another's blood.

Soft in the middle

Rose Arrowsmith DeCoux

I bless you—
wood splitter
 fire maker
 office builder
nighttime lover.
Seven years
 plus a bit
since we promised everything
in blind & total faith.
It's all been tested
  (more to come) yet
here we are,
  still married
& happily.
Better than before.
Wiser.
Kinder.
More alive &
 soft in the middle.
I am not afraid of you.
The first step love can have.

Jack and ?
Paul m. Strohm

We both made bad choices,
  everything was wrong right from the start.

Going up the hill hand in hand,
  that should never have happened.

I should have carried the pail,
  you should have stayed at the bottom.

Why we needed the darn water,
  it's still a big mystery to me.

Perhaps we were an ill-fated pair,
  destined to come tumbling down hard.

But that's all water under the bridge,
  or more accurately water spilled on the ground.

They say I will be laid up for awhile,
  a CT Scan found a subarachnoid hemorrhage in my brain.

Hope you are doing well too,
sorry but I don't remember your first name.

The neighborly doll
Matt Schumacher

at those gradeschool sleepovers
your friend's mother always
refused to put away her favorite
doll, that enormous, peculiar-looking
kewpie. why did she leave
it on the guest bed
as if insisting that it sleep
between you and your friend?
after the scary movie,
it would be there waiting
for you, no matter how or where
you turned your head. it stared right at you
both alive and dead. whether waking up
from a bad dream or sleepless,
even in the pitch black night,
with closed blinds, the plastic eyes
intensely glistening with moonlight.

Texas lovers: Sarah and Jenny
Jeston Dulin

They mention traveling to Paris, Texas and becoming artists. Their singing
isn't great and they can't paint at all but their sculptures are to-scale
duplications of WWII battlefields, constructed with painstaking attention
to detail. Perfect imitations of tiny deaths. The only inaccuracies, it would
seem, come from the repeated use of UFOs and mythological creatures.
Most scholars agree that extraterrestrials had little influence over the
Fuhrer's master plan, but Sarah and Jenny refuse to remove reptilian
features from the soldiers of the SS. They only wish that someone had told
them that verisimilitude was so important in representations of the past.

You will not be found wanting
Julia Rox

your mouth is still open
but your breath is not warm.
it comes out cold like the fog.
it is raining inside your mouth
so you cannot scream even
though it is your birthday wish.
your legs begin to fold under you like a deer.
I try to help you up by tying
silver birthday balloons to your wrists.
they look like little moons
but they will not hold you.
I will carry you home
and you will not be found wanting.
when my head is underneath your shirt
it is like being under the blankets
in my childhood bed.
after I leave
your mother will knock 3 times
on the side door
and your father will come out
to walk with her.
when they walk into the dark
you will wonder about me.
you will look at the space between your
tongue and the moon and say
ah what a terrible waste.

Yellow bone
Catherine Cimillo Cavallone

Yellow bone amid the gunsmoke—
you arise from the pyre of human chaos
and blink groggily at the modern world.

You arise from your breathing grave—
from the boarded-up mouth,
from your river of forgotten blood.

O, city of orphans,
pay your respects in secrecy.
Tend to your wounds behind the moon
and among the clouds.

Ignore the unbroken murderers
who sift through the ashes in your hair.

Ignore the last-minute looters.

Pluck the skulls from your dress
and wipe the dust from your teeth.

Yellow bone among the stars—
a vision, like a saint—
pull your memories up by the eye sockets
and you shall,
with time,
be pretty yet.

Ascent
Tamer Mostafa

in this visit
to the graveyard
i see that beneath the headstone
is a ditch
and in that ditch
is a box
and in that box
is a body
and in that body
there was a soul
a soul a body a box a ditch and
myself
alone beneath a headstone

Les rois
Phoenix Bunke

where they found our bones and yours mixed together

We heard your teeth
sink into our sister's flesh.
Not so far away, you
were pounding and scraping
at the gnawed-off jawbone
detaching the tongue with
choppy slimed strokes
fingers slipping on blood
and settling saliva.
We saw the smoke
rising from your cook-fires
over the hills. We could
smell her sweet sizzling.
Our deep brains growl to us;
our stomachs forgive.
When ever has there been
occasion to waste meat?

The last monarch butterfly
Ellyn Touchette

everyone knows the story
of the last man on earth

him sitting in his room
the knock on the door

I heard a version once:
knock comes right after

the poor bastard opens his
mouth and downs a few

capsules of cyanide and dies
like an infant wish he was here

might have known what to do
now that the flowers are gone

we go like this: bees first
crops next then the rest of the

unfortunate damned I'm
not sure where the last man is

probably been dead for a while
probably never knew what he did

probably never been called king

Another deleted Boyd
Bushman video

the moon fanglike
in a mouth
hinged with shadows

swallows everything
as we cry out

give back our stars,

— **"The animal we fear most is god"**
John Roth, page 224

ISSUE NO. 21

Visitors
Wayne F. Burke

there is a flying saucer
hovering,
a huge motherfucker
from the Planet Crouton
in galaxy triple X ten
Star Zone alpha omega delta-fy
and with ray guns enough
to destroy the city
but for some reason
doesn't,
and lands on the roof of
Dunkin' Donuts
and a little man crawls out
and goes inside
and asks for the key to
the restroom
but they won't give it to him
because
he is not a paying customer.

Company
Nate Maxson

The raccoon-people,
My own
Dark eyed
Cousins,
Out where the metal trashcans border the tree line
Have turned their old peaceful art of butter-churning
Into wooden noisemakers
Molotov-stills
An industry of firewater

Night scream
Tony Walton

This night has nothing to be ashamed of, and just staggered in this place at last call — drunken and unshaven, a kind of fuckless orgasm with no one to tuck it in bed.

This night has roamed across concrete, faced neon beer signs in liquored mirrors with hollowed eyes seeking reprieve in thirsts and pleasures sought. This night is curious. This night is weak.

This night is drenched in vodka, diazepam — forty miles from nowhere, wild and bewildered in a ceaseless thrust. This night aches. But then we see this:

Two bodies galloping against each other under cool sheets, a shudder, then a glow of silver on her snowy thigh, drying.

A bond, however fragile. Until morning when it takes flight and then it's gone?

Oh, who the hell knows, but I do know this night will stay in bed.

4 in the morning
Mark Bonica

at 4 in the morning it's just me and the truckers on the road

and the psycho killers in their minivans.

no one else is up and dressed, pants on one leg at a time, coffee sloshed.

there seem so many trucks but it's really the same number as always — just the lack of other cars makes them look like Stonehenge has decided to relocate.

there's the truck from Sysco with its cargo of Bloomin' Onions/Awesome Blossoms/Texas Roses. there's the truck from Wal-Mart with its cargo of Chinese plastic wrapped electronics. There's the BP truck with its tanks full of black paid for in blood. there's the psycho killer's minivan with its grim sacrifice carefully wrapped — a Chinese baker, perhaps who had stopped to get gas too late at night?

citizens with day jobs and for-profit criminals are all snoring — it's still yesterday's night for them.

us, we're all driving into the morning of their tomorrow (except for the Chinese baker, who will have no more tomorrows or even today).

Death cannot be proved
Bruce McRae

It's the hour of the wolf in a janitor's closet.
February is waiting at the end of the hall.
Ghost-mice are performing a danse macabre.
Here, at the institution, everything closes.
We never mention the rooms inside this room,
the dust-defying gravity, the phases of the moon.
We don't talk about the inevitable silences
or darkness pooling under a door.
We say little or nothing . . .
Established in the year Zed, the institution
is as dull as a morgue or an office meeting.
The air scarcely shifts, the files unmoved.
Our business is zero.
Now it's 4 a.m., and the roaches hold rule:
tiny tyrants throwing terrible tantrums.
Whom the ancients regarded as very old souls.
Whom the gods embraced in their ruin.

Recycled lover
Kyle Hemmings

Your recycled lover is made from your own bone and uneven pelvis,
from the days when you could not fuse properly, the torn ligaments
that only a bow-legged widow could stitch, the shark-tail of a thought
when you were naive enough to collect inkberries in a yellow-green field.
You wanted to prove that you could survive being poisoned,
that you could survive a cluster of tall needy men.

Your recycled lover and you once made a stone baby
and you never forgave each other.
Only the stone baby could not break.

The animal we fear most is god
John Roth

We mimic beasts
behind a stick-teething fire

behind the unsubtle glow-snap
of lightning pitched

overhead

the moon fanglike
in a mouth
hinged with shadows

swallows everything
as we cry out

give back our stars,
our brave morning light

not tonight he says

again & again he
takes until a savage
backlash ensues

ensures our mutual
distrust for one another

ashamed we piece together
temples from bloody stones

surround ourselves

with veiled sanctities
all so no one will see us
praying in the dark

Theatre in trance
Drew Pisarra

(You must read this poem aloud for it to work. Think of it as the spell to right the universe or an experiment in a temporal consciousness. Take a breath then begin.)

Beginning
The beginning
Of the beginning
Of the very beginning
Beginning of the very beginning
The beginning of the very beginning
The very beginning of the very beginning
The very beginning of the beginning
The very beginning of beginning
The beginning of beginning
The beginning beginning
The beginning
Beginning

(Repeat the first stanza or move on to the next. Repetition isn't inherently redundant. Language isn't necessarily thought. This poem isn't about ideas or closure. Choose.)

Ending
Ending ending
Ending of ending
The ending of ending
The ending of the ending
The very ending of the ending
The very ending of the very ending
The ending of the very ending
The ending of the ending
The ending of ending
The ending ending
Ending ending
Ending

(Only from risk rooted in desperation, in which the artist stands to look like a fool and the soul holds its invisible ground can poetry re-find a reason for being. Now move on.)

Handful of blue sky
Hillary Lyon

the middle-aged man in the hotel room
stole an umbrella from a public beach
had lips as red as sideshow devil
and as hot as coffee fresh
from the tiny microwave

he lodged that striped umbrella
between the front bucket seats
as he drove to the local dive
in his lap a rumpled paper bag
holding a brown wig he called "bunny"

he wanted you
to dress like a French maid
and scuttle across the floor
like a soft shelled crab
he wanted you

on your knees and open
mouthed like the cave of Orpheus
through which he would play
his untuned lyre and prophesy
all the troubles of the world

what you gave him
instead was a declaration
of independence disguised
as a handful of blue sky
and a shaker of salt

Pain taxonomy
Jill Khoury

Dr. Dog says
I need to
name names.
But some truths
are extradimensional.
I have climbed out
my tree, and now live
in the ozone.
Got a real
barnburner
up in my retina.
Been ejected
from one borderland
into another
uncertain
district. Woke
with welts
on my thighs
in the shape
of linden leaves.

Dark passage
Jeffrey Park

Some unseen medium – viscous, oozing like oil from deep in the tar sands – slides over the skin of our vessel, frictionless, darkly sensual, like black water from an abandoned well, like shadows from beneath the eyes of a Bedouin dancer.

And we have been journeying for so very long that we don't know, can't remember, if we are traversing the empty space between two planets, or if we are moving through the deep mantle of our own earth, buried under heavy layers of rock and soil and decaying organic matter.

And the lights we see through the viewport could be either stars or pinpricks in the earth's crust. And the sounds we hear could be the music of the celestial spheres, but they might just as well be the tortured moaning of vast continents adrift.

Deep space
Kalen Rowe

I've been abducting all the good attractive poets
So we can expat to a basement in Siberia
And freeze together. This is the only thought that ends
My loneliness. What do you do when your friends
Don't even know you? Type "kalen rowe"
Into Google. Not much comes up. You guess
I don't exist. There is little to no freedom in not existing.
First of all, you can't get any good spaceships.
You have to take the refurbished ones into orbit.
And when the autopilot ejects in the escape pod,
You have to float through Saturn's ring all by yourself.
Picture it subtle. I can't. Not for this long. Soon it will
Unsettle. Soon you turn into something else. Soon.
A glimmer in the internet. Don't make me think—
A cloud vacationing before the rain. Just sit there.
You can enjoy this crowded place while it lasts.

The bones have nothing to tell us.
Our recorders go on fingerprinting silence,
its whorls and loops
to be analyzed at a later time.
In the clearing the moon bleaches absence.

— "Ghost hunter"
Lori Lamothe, page 235

"A Wish That
Surprised Me"
Bill Wolak

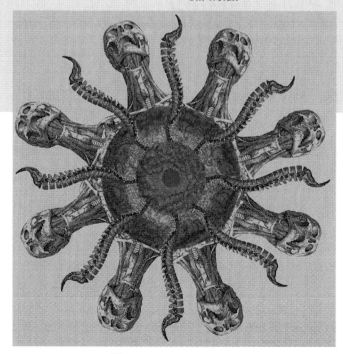

#monsters
Chloe N. Clark

In Wisconsin, two young girls stabbed
a friend repeatedly

The story made headlines,
beyond the horror,

because the girls claimed to have done it
to appease an urban legend

Slenderman has been around for only
a few years, an internet ghost

He's a figure appearing in the backgrounds
of photographs, the edges of the scene, a little
too tall and a little too thin, as if his image

has been stretched, pulled like warm taffy

People say that if Slenderman appears
behind someone then the person will die

These kinds of rules have been around
as long as story,
like frames around photos

what you can't see won't hurt you

not like girls, leading their friend
into the woods, dark and cold and green
with life, and slamming a knife
into her body, over and over, until
they thought she should be dead

In the papers, of the girls
stare straight ahead into the camera
lens, unafraid

of seeing themselves in pictures

In the hollow
Anna Sykora

they bought it cheap
the fixer-upper in the hollow
with a garden run to seed
and beat-up picket fencing
all around

tom and maria hauled
out the junk inside
and burned it in the yard
and then they tried wallpapering
weird thing the paper peeled right off
leaving oozy blotches
like fresh blood

then something went mighty wrong
the night the banging started in the cellar
doors blew open
a window shattered
it isn't safe here tom complained
this is pennsylvania maria cried
not transylvania with rotten graves

then what is that awful stink

two nights later
a pale child
rose up at the end of the bed
eyes like clotted blood
her mouth a well of darkness
howling

they fled the house
they never came back
and about a year later
it burned to the ground
and there in the smoking wreck
sheriff bounty found
the bones of a child

that's all I know
but if I were you folks
I wouldn't buy that parcel
in the hollow

Ghostlight
Paula Chew

a grotesque pest in the dark with
lines running through its head wants to splinter itself
to fucking bits because someone forgot to turn on the light
and now the space is restless,
if the constant curtain-swish and trapdoor teeth-chatter
is anything to go by.

at the turn of the light what's supposed to happen is
a dissolution of leftover selves,
a melee of souls fleeing the seep
of white slivers between blissful curtain-dark,
a silent purge of last evening's sobfest,
the same story every single goddamn night.

the vital light fends off the ghosts
of papery skin-dust and vapor, who
rattle and shudder and smolder this drafty house.
the creature in the wings loathsome shivers,
its edges flaking off to the swift burn of its skin, while
the stage peels splinter by filthy splinter.
the fear and heat of the creature, the feat
of its blind crawl up the catwalk,
the steely grip of its toes, the drip
of inky oil-blood through crowded air.
the menace weeps into its teeth. its breaths grow brief.
onstage, a little caged light ignites.

Bear the baker and harvest
David Spicer

Sal, the girl dwarf, dressed in rags.
All the easier to grope and screw
her, Bear the Baker, grizzly huge,
bragged. I love to keep them
blindfolded for hours in sunlight.
He discarded her, his first ex-wife,
because of club feet. Bear sagged
in the hammock touching the ground.
He altered women I'd bring him,
forced them to waltz. They wore
a different wig every day, ate meals
of pretzels and a vodka drink, Magic Debris.
I delivered him ten beauties who died
of various maladies: breast cancer,
dementia, diabetes. When they tried
to flee, he forced them to eat powdered glass,
hog-tied them to steel beams in his basement.
Nice enough to supply blankets.
Harvest, orange-haired scarecrow, escaped
in a customer's truck. Two years later, dressed
as Mata Hari, she returned to Bear, who stared
at this magnificence, called her his ski champion.
Powerless, he plunged into depression,
visited shrinks, failed to flourish.
One day Harvest built a sawed-off,
blew off Bear's head, stuck it on the wall
with his other trophies. She spared me,
the best damned taxidermist in the county.

A primitive plant
Midori Chen

the rafters of the house unraveled on the equinox
the color of old prison denim, her little house on the—
worm-chewed, worm-spat, tepid coffee from secondhand grounds—
prairie, dogs with mangled throats prowling the edge
digging up the dirt-soaked porch
webs and white chalk underneath
an incarcerated clavicle
some missing posters: *ten pints of blood if found return to*
hair— mats of it— does hair rot? if so how?
(ask Jane Doe, her vertebrae, her mandible
worm-chewed, worm-spat
an infant raccoon's rattle)
middle of the earth, middle of the day
flashfloods wash the evidence away
and the rafter *breaks*
(no infant sparrows survive the fall)
for coyotes, ravens to feast on the remains

Ghost happy hour
Christopher Woods

Each night the same. A few scotches in the dusty library, furniture shrouded
in white sheets. Ethereal music from upstairs. Then, the malt coursing in your
veins, leave the house, go down the brick walk to the old boathouse, place of
secrets and one very unfortunate accident. Shadows all around, some ahead
as if leading the way, or from behind, following, a nightly migration of ghosts
in moonlight. How the accident happened leads back to the embrace, stronger
than anticipated, hard lips against your own, the pressure you felt in your thighs.
And though you were dizzy with the attention and the risk of it all, he being
such an old and close family friend, you felt something give way. Your legs, all
shaky and rubberlike, deserted you. With a gasp you fell into the berth, hit your
head on the stern of the sailboat and disappeared, unaware that above you
the old friend was stepping back, from the water, from you, and ultimately, from
responsibility.

Robert
Matt Schumacher

i'm the life-sized doll filled with straw
in my white sailor's suit, clutching my stuffed lion.
a family maid who knew my voodoo
gave me to a child, robert "gene" otto.
the child would live by my new law.
the child soon called me by his first name
as if we were inseparable twin brothers.
i went everywhere he did. but his mother interfered—
she overheard two different voices
shouting in gene's bedroom. she found mutilated toys,
overturned furniture when they broke in.
gene screamed robert did it! mom and dad
merely laughed at the toy scapegoat.
most humans don't know how my power grows,
its looming shadows. giddy inhuman laughter
echoed through those rooms. and yes, the doll
glimpsed hurrying upstairs, moving
from window to window—that was me.
older, gene inherited the mansion after his parents died.
as if faithful, I stood by his side,
black button eyes sewn to his paintings
in the turret bedroom. gene married.
his new wife nearly fainted
when she met me. she complained that he and I
had grown too close. she locked me in the attic. how traumatic
when that woman soon went mad and died.
she learned who gene's real friend was.
i survived to sit at his deathbed.
i outlived the whole family in the end.
did I kill them? you'll never know.
there was no trial, but i'm imprisoned
in the fort east martello museum in key west.
i put a curse on those who snap photos
without asking first, those who don't show respect.
later, they write the letters taped to my glass case.
they beg me to lift my hexes. after hours,
when the museum's closed, i never tire of the fun:
i laugh and read aloud repeatedly the pleas
of weeping fools who plead for my forgiveness.

The bone
Stephen Bunch

Where did you find it?
In a field near my father's house.

Did the flesh still cling to it?
It was picked clean, bleached, dry.

Were you afraid?
I picked it up.

What did you feel?
Revulsion and pride.

What will you do with it?
I'll braid my hair with it

or hold it when I sleep.
May I touch it?

Never, you may
never touch it.

Ghost hunter
Lori Lamothe

—at the Rutland Prison Camp Ruins

We ask questions of grass,
darkness, an owl's screech.
As for the dead, they don't
comment, forward all inquiries
to the stones that aren't
there. Graves unmarked,
lives nameless, crimes
forgotten or erased
off the spirit maps
we've shoved into back pockets
of skepticism. Someone
wants to know if they're at last
at peace, if they've found
redemption or remorse,
if the stopped voices
floated up from dried flowers
and coaxed them at last
toward understanding or maybe
just memory, just that.

The bones have nothing to tell us.
Our recorders go on fingerprinting silence,
its whorls and loops
to be analyzed at a later time.
In the clearing the moon bleaches absence.

Devil in a blue dress
Nancy Flynn

She's blue
the I that turned into this
you.   This I, an I-
oh, you.
Easier to ad
-dress, to dis/appear
in a dress.
        Simpler
to split the atom
-ized or (even) the atomizer of your/
my
choice perfume.
        You, on the other
hand, back
-ward leaning, lured
memories, stick your
tongue out—who has the upper
hand? Hear.
*

        Here.
                Your eyes
used to be blue. Envied, shift
to green. The crystal gaze would say
impure. The bluest ai
yi yi,   do stet away—
the Is   the yous
the eyes   the ewes
the poet Ai   the use.
*

I
am speaking to
the you,
the one I ceded my
lost/last voice,
I—
better entrusted to you?

You with that loveliest

oo & leading, yielding
Y. Of the why versus
I don't like the way a mouth must
shape, grimace
the I, more ai yi yi
this I
this I used
this I used to want,
crave see,
be seen—the eye beheld,
others who'd cast the
eye you/I, me
up.
But now I've turned to
you, historic
you who used to
do/be that,
a cardboard cut,
scissors in a
hand.
No more the I, the in & out
a door, that skeleton key,
the glassed-in porch.
Where you sat.
Where I watched.
Where we cleaved to split.
Where we shed, we
left, two
skins. Excused from
chatter, blast/bombast.
The tried & trying,
true. Tired now?
It's true.
*

I have been teaching myself to want.
You have been wondering if it would
stick.
The riddle outside her
            blind, my blinds, your bind, the
long
            un/winding road.

A self that's split & I who eyes about
the world, first person claimed but
(still) thinking
you. You that's the eye
seen third and, I
who wisely took the seat in
back, set out to watch
this reconnoitered
you, that you who did it—
risky
stumbling
fell.
Her solo path.
Yours, too. The wringing out of
words do ring, mere
hands   do script & fail
me
too & erase
you.
*

The bluest eye
The bluest I
The bluest you who blew
in blustery & blessed,
a blister on the bruise that's you,
my shins, her high high
shoes.
The eye/I is an unreliable, an
oracle, the I is a
dunce & a stumble, a
butcher baker candlestick
maker, rapscallion thief. The I is a pole
with
hat & shoes. You, oh you, the you is a
woo. The ewe is a wolf in curled-right
wool.
Life is a short eye/short   I
blink.
For O, she's
blue the I that's
turned,

turned into this:
this,
you.

*"Devil in a Blue Dress" borrows its
title from the novel by Walter Mosley.

The barricade tape on 111th street
Sarah Key

POLICE LINE DO NOT CROSS   the glass and steel tower
where I live since it razed a donut shop and bodega gone with the
turn
of a century that is REFORZADO   REINFORCED   yellow plastic remnants
made by Empire not to fray into   bangs I heard last night   three or
 four
CAUTION   CUIDADO   CAUTION pops at two in the morning the
dreaming
hour no concern of mine until I got the LINE from my super that a 17-year-old
boy
DO NOT CROSS was shot in the head   D.O.A.   another white outline settled
in the dust of so many   fallen to the ground   what if the chalked specters
rose to
         LINE
up the   POLICE   what if we could see how many   DO NOT ENTER
history
died in that one spot how would this crime scene look with all the   CAUTION
used
up for
tape my block a yellow web
the dead too thick to CROSS

Regarding the serial killers in boston
Kalen Rowe

Yah there was lots of screaming.
But there's always screaming right?
I mean how can you tell you know?
How can you really tell the difference?
Between screaming and laughter?
There were lots of kids in the apartments.
You could hear them coming home.
Waiting in the morning for the bus.
Maybe it was the kids who really knows.
One time I saw a guy in my window.
He was more like a kid but an old kid.
He was hauling some big black bag.
Not dragging it or anything just hauling.
Like it was too big to be neatly carried.
I only saw it because I was doing squats.
I like to stare out the window when I'm squatting.
Just shirtless with gym short-shorts on.
Weird I know but no one can really see.
I mean what was in that bag though?
Why didn't he let it drag on the ground?
Like what would it have sounded like?

In my time
Rose Aiello Morales

This is
the time of dying,
graves dug
scarce before
they're occupied,
earth that crumbles
in my hands
that fill and fill
remind me
"Soon, soon"
I'll join this
party
with the grubs
and worms,
and oh so many
waiting
on my arrival.

"Hierophant"
Nico Rico

ISSUE NO. 23

The ligatures tighten. I've been here my entire life ...

— **"The Convict"**
Cameron Morse, page 246

Cannibal suicide
Willie Smith

I poured a finger of scotch into a coffee cup
and ate the cup and licked up the spilled scotch
and ate the mouth of the fifth down to the neck and
was wolfing the table leg, when
mother came in to iron some bugs out
of her pocket calculator
and couldn't help but notice the ruined fifth,
the cup nowhere and the table wobbly
on three legs. She threatened to knuckle down
and hand it to me,
but I trumped her rump,
tugged the table leg out of my throat
and clubbed her to death. Blood spattered
the venetian blinds and mother slumped
to the foot of the refrigerator.

I threw up a window and sat on a foot stool and
reswallowed the table leg
and munched on the arm of a chair
till I was stuffed, then jerked down the wallphone
and ate out the mouthpiece
and considered sucking the news off the tv,
but decided instead to put the mouth
of a firearm to my temple
and pray

Jersey gothic
Kayla Bashe

beautiful boy lashes himself to a microphone in a storm, counts out self-blame for woven static, his bones equivalent to knives carapace reflected armor with a jagged red edge, polishing his boots with scabs. sidewalk crack silent lips. stifled hurricane eyes.

do you remember when you were twelve and I was eight, lakeside summer sick with stone-fruit, twined rope knot bracelets, sunset fizzed like lemonade when you guided fireflies into my hands listen: neither of us knew how to spell fear there is a man in a cabin locked these fifty years and his eyes are lost marbles, his fingers are snakes. we drank gasoline juice in swim trunks stapled to splintering chairs. he was the shadows of dead trees on your window at night. Listen: it should be me with algae for eyes, wandering forever barefoot over pine cones and gravel. My fingers wound through fishing hooks. My gravestone teeth. except you pushed me out his front door, your hands more ungentle than I'd ever known.

(I sat up all night with your changeling corpse; your parents didn't notice how the seaweed mocked your eyelashes.)

hear me through the cracked ice in that winter lake, hear me through the scrawled palimpsest of your skin. If the cabins awake and the pine trees catch fire: keep watchful, caged barbed-wire boy. My sneakers still slap the fastest in all of New Jersey. Here is my slingshot and the memory of raspberries. My glow-stick crown. If the drowned man tries to touch me my tattoos will melt through his hands. I've got the snarlvines of forest fire sunsets, an armada of wild geese and tadpoles to steal you back.

I'll tell your parents, here is your son; seaweed-scented with a wounded raptor's eyes, chestnut-stained nails, hands cold enough to steady close. Feed him your casserole. Wash all the softest mint-green sheets. I'll point out the castaway boy in the man's rolling voice, salvaged and mine. How we've both drifted home.

The filleted mermaid
Hannah Rose Neuhauser

Her turquoise tail shimmies and spirals to neon noise indifferent to the eyes filleting skin from ribs. The moon helps her swallow a spoonful of bitter memory. Her bones blade through her back, scalpels once sharpened on a bathroom door as fingers plucked scales into grout—fallen stars left to cool, their color bleeding into water dripped from clean hands. Ink jetted through her translucent torso like a celaphod's smokescreen. Blue echoes eclipsed her breasts, leaving luminous crescents—birthing modesty. She dragged the shards of beer bottles before removal to watch the glittered red pearls form. Every night she casts herself back into brimming floor, tongue clinging to the salt shaken from tilted glass.

Error, (I have been disconnected)
Khadija Hussain

I've been using the internet, lately.
Googling feelings, specifically,
is it normal to cry in every airport.
I want help, are you like me? Connect
me, but not too much. I don't want to know
how you're afraid of dying, how everyone is,
like how my father's father died, like how I've never known
because I've never asked.
Professional tells me, "You could benefit
from something new." We could all
benefit from something new.
Hey, Google, *I'm growing out of the people I loved.*
In my neighborhood we talk, drink
breathe the same. See, best friend, I'm ice cubing
out of our previous existence,
Tell me about your carpets,
your coffee preference, your SATs, only don't cry,
all I've ever learned is that we're closer
when we're strangers.   Google, save me
a bite to eat— I won't make it
home for dinner tonight.

Acid bath confession letter
Justin Holliday

(To John Wayne Gacy)

Place me inside the envelope though I am naked
except for unintelligible scribbles. Seal me in
the secret spit thirty-three men already know

that you have defiled bodies; your body
is a knife, tearing with hands, throats
collapse. You want to clear the air,

the moldering crawlspace where rot breathes in,
where time calcifies under quicklime,
and faces stretch in frozen masks,

choking on dirty underwear, screams unheard.
Not out of the closet but below ground,
you could not stop yourself.

Stamp me with your signet, a burden
I am willing to bear only to be torn
open again. First, just write

I did it. List names, all of the names.
Before you burn me with wax,
I see your fingers crawling

back inside, unfolding me, smearing me
with fast food stains as you walk me
over to the motionless ones,

drop me down, and pour more chemicals
where we will all dissolve
as your balloon body

floats to the next boy.

The cannery
Holly Day

the heads line the wall of her basement
like pickles or tomatoes in clear glass jars
tiny strips of paper scotch-taped to the lids
first and last names covered in a thin sheen of
sticky dust, sometimes, she arranges the jars

alphabetically, sometimes by last name, sometimes
by first, a confusing mix of ancient and newer loves
young faces mixed with old. Sometimes
she lines the jars up by date, from the very first kiss
to the last bad blind grope in the back of a car

but that arrangement always makes her sad, reminds her
of how hard it is for an older woman
to find love.

It's like you were never even here
Mike Salgado

There is an effect that sets in when a person leaves this place of white and attempted sterility. The microscopes will long for your eyes.

Myself and those before you called it the effect of, "it's like you were never even here." After a week setting off from the halls of red pathological waste boxes, dry ice and senselessness we will forget you were ever here to begin with. We'll only recall a name and some attributes, not the good ones. The scalpels could never slice those away.

Yourself, you may think back to that cramped office with Ryan each time you smell cigarette smoke and see an energy drink. Energy better spent in the present. Let your mind be iodine-swabbed to a sterile yellow.

The convict
Cameron Morse

A nineteen-year-old girl
tied to a cemetery tree. Look up
he says, and she does it: dark morning

clouds adrift, scrawling across
the sky their illegible script.

Wind slips like a razorblade
over the strop
twisting branches. Rainwater

gurgles into the ground.
The ligatures tighten.
I've been here my entire life

looking up, losing feeling
feeling bound
to the body and its habits,

to the earth and its laws
to its laws and its
lawlessness.

Renfield's syndrome
KG Newman

My uncle used to smoke hash
and walk the high beams
of Detroit, no harness,
and on late-night TV I see
cops with their PB&J sandwich halves,
their steaming coffee, standing around
the taped-off crime scene
of a dead body, a dead mouse,
a wilted rosebush.
It's not that I don't have strength,
it's that I tend to write my
strong foolish words
on yellow notebook paper—
I'd walk the high beams
but no amount of hash
is ever enough. I'd love to duck
under the caution tape,
squat down to inspect
the carcasses, flick my
cigarette, say something
Law & Order-worthy,
prick my finger on the final stem
with any remnant of color to it
and suck the blood
oozing from my wound.
There are other ways to survive
but I've never learned.
There are other ways
to get high. This one barely works.

Bright, with the glory of all (to be read at my funeral)
Andrew Chmielowiec

and, of all my broken parts:

the bruised and worn,
the reddened,
the sagging,
and the almost-falling-off,

i will regret not a one;

i have worn them proudly,
like medals of honor,

and even hidden
underneath socks and sweaters
they have shined, bright,

with the glory of all.

(...that i have stepped on,
that i have crashed into,

been burned by,
bitten, sickened, stuck,

and the few reminders
that i have left myself...)

there is a glowing
that i would not trade
for a second chance.

i will take it with me.

and, i am taking all of it.

Once upon a bicycle
Veronica McDonald

Once upon a bicycle,
I fell and scraped my knee.
The stranger came upon me
and bellowed, "Come with me."
My bike was left in the dirt
where weeds poked through the spokes.
The metal rusted through the silver,
the leather cracked, the reflector broke.
He wrapped me all in bandages,
my toes to head to chest.
Only my bloody knee was exposed,
the blinding crimson expressed
all that I could not;
my mouth was bandaged, too.
"I want my orange bicycle,"
I tried to say to the man in blue.
"Don't move," he said. "Don't try to talk.
This is serious work I do."
I hungered for the handle bars,
the ground rushing past my seat,
the air biting at my lungs and face,
long grass whipping at my feet.
He's tying me with bandages,
long and white, around the bed.
"This won't hurt. With any luck,
you'll never hurt again."
Once upon a bicycle,
I fell and scraped my knee.
The blood is spilling on the bed
as the stranger watches me.

Tundra
Anton Yakovlev

You've had enough.
You plan a trip to the tundra.

You want to stand
on a barren Arctic shore
before an invisible ocean
on a moonless night,
mindful of nothing besides
your scratchy coat.

—

Death comes in, wearing mittens over his heart.
His ribcage protrudes through his torso.
He rattles the air, eager to start a skirmish,
only to retire into a hammock
and swing his bony legs in the air.

Death is ill. Death waves
the world's most terminally boring flag.

"Hey Death," you say, "can I make your day
sweeter somehow? Stop sulking,
Death! Make angels!"

—

Your lot in life is skydiving with the skylarks,
pomegranate slushie in hand.

My lot in life is being your commissar,
healing your warts,
being your bud.

Every morning, we get on the train together,
trade lychee custards.
Our alchemy is never to say goodbye.

We spin our vinyls infinitely,
and that's what fortifies us.

—

Don't fall for Death's lovesong,
steel yourself against the derecho of fruit flies
that make holes in our hulls.

Stave off the tundra.
Beware the feathers of its cardinals.
Linger here;
dare sin and repent.

Scan the ocean
like it's a farmer's market
and hook the tilapias of the morning.

Indigo winter
Chris 'Irish Goat' Knodel

They buried me alive, in a casket — for a secret.
Endless hours, I have shivered,
and stared into a sea of iridescent silk.

My air is thinning.

My final moments will be spent alone in a midnight blue cell;
my worth measured in the ohms I generate trembling.
I am my own fading battery.

No one will come.

I am tied to the frigid womb of a dead mother.
A birth that will never be.
An inmate in this indigo winter.

My eternal season.

CONTRIBUTOR BIOS

Alex Brown was raised in the southern U.S. but graduated from Utah Valley University with a BS in Behavioral Science. He now lives in Sweden where he is re-awakening his admiration of the written word. He uses writing as a way to make his ideas and the subconscious of his dreams become more accessible. You can follow him on his blog at http://peripheraldiving.wordpress.com. (He also confessed that he loved Animal Collective and all it's reincarnations. I'm pretty sure that would qualify Alex Brown as a hipster, but I don't want to get sued for libel.)

Alex Ehrhardt is a graduate of the College of Wooster, currently living and writing in the Boston metro area. If you're ever in town, he'll probably be reading on an open mic. He has had fiction published in the Goliard and memoir in the first issue of Maps for Teeth. His poetry is previously unpublished.

Alicia A. Curtis lives in Lawrenceville, GA with a photographer, a cat and ten fish. She enjoys bird-watching, divination, and listening to the wind. Her poetry has most recently appeared or is forthcoming in "Gothic Poems and Flash Fiction", "Abramelin", "This Great Society", and "The Last Man Anthology".

Ali Znaidi lives in Redeyef, Tunisia. He graduated with a BA in Anglo-American Studies in 2002. He teaches English at Tunisian public secondary schools. He writes poetry and has an interest in literature, languages, and literary translation. He likes to smoke while sipping tea with mint. His pen aspires to write something white on a black cloud before the rain falls. His work has appeared in The Bamboo Forest. Two tiny poems are due to be published respectively in April and May in fortunates.org. He writes flash fiction for the Six Sentence Social Network — http://sixsentences.ning.com/profile/AliZnaidi.

Amber Decker is an undergraduate student majoring in English literature. Her writing has been featured internationally in numerous publications, both in print and online, and her latest full-length collection of poems is Lost Girls. Currently, she lives with her husband in the eastern panhandle of West Virginia where she watches werewolf movies and wastes countless hours playing video games. She blogs semi-regularly at http://roughverse.wordpress.com.

Amit Parmessur hails from the heavenly island of Mauritius. Aged 28, he has been writing for the past 8 years. He has been accepted and appeared in several magazines including Ann Arbor Review, Yes Poetry, Leaf Garden Press, Burnt Bridge, Calliope Nerve, Catapult to Mars, Censored Poets, Clockwise Cat, Clutching at Straws, Damazine, Gloom Cupboard, Heavy Hands Ink, LITSNACK, Mad Swirl, Orchard Press Mysteries, Puffin Circus, Shalla Magazine, Shot Glass Journal, The Camel Saloon, The Houston Literary Review, The Scrambler and Word Slawamong others. He is also busy with Golden Apple Ezine, of which he is one of the editors.

Amy Elisabeth Olson is a twenty-something suburban refugee armed with a BA in English, electronic music and her grandmother's silver.

Andrew Chmielowiec lives in Seattle, Washington, and most certainly does believe in ghosts. he has self-published a chapbook by the name of "sir baden powell patrol award winners, 2003-04," and has a modest amount of short poems featured in small publications. his current writing can be found at sillyandrew.tumblr.com.

Andrew J. Stone is a storyteller and words express what he sees in the world. Without mankind's dark lusts, his writing would not exist. He tries to expose the dark layer surrounding the heart in order to make sense of this world. His hope is that his poetry will enable other individuals to do the same.

Anastasia Chew is an eighteen year old vagabond who has completed several halves of novels and often forgets to eat. Despite these non-accomplishments, a jazz ensemble serenades her every morning en route to the subway.

Anna Sykora has been an attorney in NYC and teacher of English in Germany, where she resides with her patient husband and three enormous cats. To date she has placed 388 poems in the small press and 141 stories. Writing is her joy.

Anne Butler, a Virginia native, is currently an Los Angeles-based actor/singer who fell in love with poetry many years ago, while studying theater in San Francisco. On the corner of Bush Street and Grant Avenue, to the tune of lone a street saxophonist, she picked up The Words Under the Words by Naomi Shihab Nye and read every word. Now, in addition to reading, she writes! When she is not on stage or agonizing in front of a computer screen, she enjoys long walks, tea lattes, and the more-than-occasional X-Files re-run.

Annie Neugebauer is a short story writer, novelist, and award-winning poet. She has work appearing or forthcoming in Wichita Falls Literature and Art Review, Six Sentences, Texas Poetry Calendar 2011, Voices de la Luna, Versifico, Collections I, Ardent!, The Stray Branch, Dark Horizons, Eunoia Review, and Encore. Annie is the President of the North Branch Writers' Critique Group as well as the Vice President of the Denton Poets' Assembly. She lives in Denton, Texas with her husband Kyle and two cats, Buttons and Snaps. You can visit her at www.WordsByAnnie.com.

Anthony Jones is a writer and basketball coach living in Brooklyn. His work has appeared (or is scheduled to appear) in Westwind, The Furnace Review, The Montreal Review, PANK Magazine, Storychord, Poetry Quarterly, The Write Room, Amphibi.us, and Orion Headless. He was also the 2007 recipient of UCLA's Ruth Brill Scholarship, awarded for outstanding achievement in creative writing. These days, he's working on his first novel, which is based primarily on his experiences with ex-girlfriends and John

Wayne movies. Some days he feels like everything in the story is falling into place, other days he can't write because he's worried that he doesn't have enough friends on Facebook.

Originally from Moscow, Russia, **Anton Yakovlev** studied filmmaking and poetry at Harvard University. He is the author of chapbooks Neptune Court (The Operating System, 2015) and The Ghost of Grant Wood (Finishing Line Press, 2015). His work is published or forthcoming in The New Yorker, The Hopkins Review, Fulcrum, American Arts Quarterly, Measure, The Nervous Breakdown and elsewhere. He has also directed several short films.

Becca Thorne is currently based in Leicester, UK, where she works from home in her spare room studio, creating hand printed pieces in linocut, screenprint and wood engraving. The above linocut was inspired by "Red Within" by Steve Taose.

Ben John Smith is a Melbourne based poet who get qweezy every time he hears the word poet. If he had a bigger set of balls he would move to Thailand and be done with all the bullshit that the non-Thailand people get up to.

Bill Gainer has contributed to the literary scene as a writer, editor, promoter, publicist, publisher and poet. He continues to read and work with a wide range of poets and writers, including readings on KUSF radio, S.F. with Punk-Rocker Patti Smith and performances with California Poet Laureate, Al Young. Gainer is nationally published and remains a sought after reader, preview him at billgainer.com.

Bill Wolak is a poet, photographer, and collage artist. His collages have been published in The Annual, Peculiar Mormyrid, Danse Macabre, Dirty Chai, Hermeneutic Chaos Literary Journal, Lost Coast Review, Yellow Chair Review, Otis Nebula, and Horror Sleaze Trash. He has just published his twelfth book of poetry entitled Love Opens the Hands with Nirala Press. Recently, he was a featured poet at The Mihai Eminescu International Poetry Festival in Craiova, Romania. Mr. Wolak teaches Creative Writing at William Paterson University in New Jersey.

Brad Liening lives in Minneapolis. He's the author of Ghosts and Doppelgangers (Lowbrow Press).

Pushcart-nominee **Bruce McRae** is a Canadian musician with over 800 publications, including Poetry.com and The North American Review. His first book, 'The So-Called Sonnets' is available from the Silenced Press website or via Amazon books. To hear his music and view more poems visit his website: www.bpmcrae.com, or 'TheBruceMcRaeChannel' on Youtube.

Cameron Morse taught and studied in China. He is currently an MFA candidate at UMKC and lives with his wife, Lili, in Blue Springs, Missouri. His work has been or will be published in I-70 Review, TYPO, Otis Nebula, Sleet, Steam Ticket, Referential

Magazine, Rufous City Review, Small Print Magazine, Two Hawks Quarterly, First Class Literary Magazine, Phantom Kangaroo, Cha and District Lit.

Caroline Misner is a graduate of Sheridan College of Applied Arts & Technology with a diploma in Media Arts Writing. She was nominated for the prestigious Writers' Trust/McClelland & Stewart Journey Anthology Prize in 2009, as well a Pushcart Prize in 2010. In 2004 her novella received Honorable Mention in the L. Ron Hubbard Writers of the Future Contest. A short story was also a finalist in the same contest. A novel, The Glass Cocoon was a semi-finalist for the William Faulkner-William Wisdom Award the following year.

Cassandra de Alba's work has appeared or is forthcoming in Red Lightbulbs, Illuminati Girl Gang, Strange Horizons, and Drunken Boat, among other publications. Her most recent chapbooks are called Bloodlust (No Spaceships Allowed) and Special Bitch Academy. She lives in Massachusetts and blogs at outsidewarmafghans. tumblr.com.

Catfish McDaris is a journeyman New Mexican bricklayer in Milwaukee. He has been published widely for 20 years. His most infamous chap is Prying with Jack Micheline & Bukowski. His works have been in NYQ, Rattle, Louisiana Review, Chiron, Haight Ashbury, Pearl, Main St. Rag, Slipstream, & Cafe Review. His last big reads were in NYC & The Shakespeare & Co. Bookstore in Paris.

Catherine Cimillo Cavallone is a teacher and poet. Her work has appeared in Four Walls, Sensations Magazine, The Rift Arts Forum Publication, Beyond the Rift-Poets of the Palisades, Red River Review and has work forthcoming in Red Wheel Barrow and Oddville Press. She lives in New Jersey with her husband, George and son, Michael.

Catherine Owen has published nine haunted collections of poems and one of prose. Other spooky facts about her can be found on her website: www.catherineowen.org. This poem is from Cineris, a manuscript dedicated to her spouse who died in 2010.

As a compulsive biter, **Chad Redden's** teeth marks have been recorded on many shoulders throughout the continental United States. As a writer, his work has appeared in analog and digital publications such as Booth, Escape into Life, New Wave Vomit, and Red Lightbulbs. He also edits NAP. NAPLITMAG.COM.

Changming Yuan, 4-time Pushcart nominee and author of Chansons of a Chinaman, grew up in rural China and published several monographs before moving to Canada. With a PhD in English, Yuan currently teaches in Vancouver and has had poetry appearing in nearly 550 literary publications worldwide, including Asia Literary Review, Best Canadian Poetry, BestNewPoemsOnline, Exquisite Corpse, London Magazine, Paris/Atlantic, Poetry Kanto, SAND and Taj Mahal Review.

Born in Boston, MA and raised in Savannah, GA, **Cheri Anne's** speech is divided as well as every other aspect of her outlook. As a trolley tour guide by day and student/writer by night, her super powers tend to be most drained. She's never really understood "courtesy" or "hospitality" anyway. She lives a double life shrouded by science and mapped pamphlets where she can only think in verse. She has been published by TUCK magazine as the first contributor to be published under both categories within the same issue, and by Pill Hill Press, Wicked East Press, and Danse Macabre du Jour magazine.

Chloe N. Clark's work appears in Bombay Gin, Booth, Sleet, Wyvern, and more. She writes about magicians, ghosts, and doughnuts in equal proportions. Follow her @ PintsNCupcakes

Chris 'Irish Goat' Knodel is an author, poet and ultra-distance runner in San Antonio, TX. His poetry and short fiction have been featured in/by Alba, Allegro Poetry Magazine, Ealain, Haiku Journal, Grey Wolfe Publishing, Highfield Press, Icarus Down Review, Kind of a Hurricane Press, Pretty Owl Poetry, The Wolfian, The Write Place at the Write Time, Writer's Quibble, Yellow Chair Review, Ygdrasil, Zimbell House Publishing, & Zodiac Review. He can be easily spotted by his kilt, tattoos and six inch, flaming-red, Van Dyke goatee.

Chris Kobylinsky is studying English literature as a graduate student at Western Connecticut State University. He has been a writer of poetry and stories for as long as he can remember. His writing is not only inspired by his many literary heroes — such as Shakespeare, Homer, Emily Dickinson, Wallace Stevens, and Gerard Manley Hopkins — it is also inspired by the hay bale sprinkled pastures, the stone wall–laced forests, and the abandoned silos of New England. Chris has recently completed his first young adult novel and is pursuing a career in publishing.

Christopher Woods is a writer, teacher and photographer who lives in Houston and Chappell Hill, Texas. He has published a novel, THE DREAM PATCH, a prose collection, UNDER A RIVERBED SKY, and a book of stage monologues for actors, HEART SPEAK. His work has appeared in THE SOUTHERN REVIEW, NEW ENGLAND REVIEW, NEW ORLEANS REVIEW, COLUMBIA and GLIMMER TRAIN, among others. His photographs can be seen in his gallery -http://christopherwoods.zenfolio.com/. He is currently compiling a book of photography prompts for writers, FROM VISION TO TEXT.

Christy Effinger teaches English at a community college in Indianapolis. Her writing has appeared in Southern Indiana Review, Word Riot, elimae, Dark Sky Magazine, All Things Girl, Cezanne's Carrot, EarthSpeak Magazine, Girls with Insurance, Melusine, and elsewhere.

Cindy Rinne creates art and writes in San Bernardino, CA. She is a founding member of PoetrIE, an Inland Empire based literary community. Her work appeared or is forthcoming in Lyre, Lyre, Cactus Heart Press, The Wayfarer, Twelve Winters Press, The Lake, Revolution House, Soundings Review, East Jasmine Review, Linden Ave. Literary Journal, The Gap Toothed Madness, and others. She has a poetry manuscript, The Feather Ladder and has written and illustrated a chapbook called, Rootlessness. www.fiberverse.com.

Claire Joanne Huxham's fiction has appeared in Monkeybicycle and The Molotov Cocktail. She lives just outside Bristol, UK, and teaches English at a local college. She can often be found obsessing over Buffy and Battlestar Galactica, cats, sushi and cheese. This is her first poetry publication. http://clairejoannehuxham.blogspot.com/

C.M. Humphries is the author of forthcoming horror novel Excluded, and his shorter works appear in Full of Crow Quarterly, Fashion for Collapse, among others. He is a graduate of Ball State University (Muncie, IN). In another life, he walks around the night.

Cynthia Linville teaches in the English Department at California State University, Sacramento and is active in the local poetry scene. She is Managing Editor of Convergence: an online journal of poetry and art. Her book of collected poems, The Lost Thing (2012), is available from Cold River Press.

Daniel Romo is an MFA candidate at Queens University of Charlotte, but represents the LBC. His poetry can be found in Fogged Clarity, MiPoesias, Scythe, Praxilla, and elsewhere. His first book of poetry, Romancing Gravity, is forthcoming from Pecan Grove Press. More of his writing can be found at danielromo.wordpress.com.

David Russomano graduated in 2006 with a BA in creative writing from Messiah College. His poetry has been featured in Write from Wrong, This Great Society, and Red Booth Review. It is also scheduled to appear in an upcoming issue of Women in REDzine. He currently teaches English in Turkey.

David McLean is Welsh but has lived in Sweden since 1987. He lives there on an island in a large lake called Mälaren, very near to Stockholm, with woman, cats, and a couple of large black and tan dogs. He is an atheist, an anarchist and generally disgusting. He has a BA in History from Balliol, Oxford, and an MA in philosophy, taken much later and much more seriously studied for, from Stockholm. Up to date details of well over a thousand poems in various zines over the last three years or so and several available books and chapbooks, including three print full lengths, a few print chapbooks, and a free electronic chapbook, are at his blog at http://mourningabortion.blogspot.com.

David Spicer has had poems accepted by or published in American Poetry Review, Ploughshares, The Curly Mind, Slim Volume, Yellow Chair Review, Jersey Devil Press, and elsewhere. He is the author of one full-length collection and four chapbooks and is the former editor of raccoon, Outlaw, and Ion Books. He lives in Memphis, Tennessee.

Daniel M. Shapiro is a schoolteacher who lives in Pittsburgh. He is the author of three chapbooks: The 44th-Worst Album Ever (NAP Books, forthcoming), Trading Fours (Pudding House Press, forthcoming), and Teeth Underneath (FootHills Publishing). He is the co-author of Interruptions (Pecan Grove Press), a collection of collaborations with Jessy Randall. His poems have appeared or are forthcoming in Chiron Review, Gargoyle, RHINO, Sentence, and Forklift, Ohio. His poetry website is http://littlemyths-dms.blogspot.com/

David Tomaloff (b. 1972) is a writer, photographer, musician, and all around bad influence. His work has appeared in fine publications such as Mud Luscious, >kill author, Thunderclap!, HOUSEFIRE, Prick of the Spindle, DOGZPLOT, elimae, and many more. He is the author of the chapbooks, Olifaunt (The Red Ceilings Press, 2011), EXIT STRATEGIES (Gold Wake Press, 2011) and MESCAL NON-PALINDROME CINEMA (Ten Pages Press, 2011). He resides in the form of ones and zeros at: davidtomaloff.com

Dawn Schout's poetry has appeared in Breadcrumb Scabs, Down in the Dirt, Fogged Clarity, Foliate Oak Literary Journal, Glass: A Journal of Poetry, Midwest Literary Magazine, Muscle & Blood Literary Journal, Poetry Quarterly, The Centrifugal Eye, Tipton Poetry Journal, and a dozen other publications. She lives near Lake Michigan.

Denise Rodriguez received her MFA in Poetry from Texas State University in San Marcos, TX, and her B.A. of Arts from The University of Texas at Austin. Her work has appeared in Room Magazine, A River and Sound Review, VAYAVYA Magazine, The Doctor T. J. Eckleburg Review, Kweli Journal, The Pedestal Magazine, and other fine places. She was a participant in the 30/30 Project for Tupelo Press during the month of August in 2013.

Denny E. Marshall has had art, poetry, and fiction published. Recent credits include art and poetry in Stinkwaves #2 and Night to Dawn #24. He does have a website with previously published works.

Donal Mahoney lived and worked most of his life in Chicago. He now lives in St. Louis, Missouri, which despite an epidemic of drive-by shootings is probably a safer place to reside. His poems have appeared in the U.S. and abroad in both print and online journals. He still hears voices in the night when he rises to hover but they no longer speak English. Sadly, he speaks not a word of Old Slavonic.

Dorene O'Brien is a fiction writer and a teacher of creative writing. She has won numerous awards for her fiction, including the Red Rock Review's Mark Twain Award for Short Fiction, the New Millennium Writings Fiction Award, the Iowa Literary Award the Chicago Tribune Nelson Algren Award and the international Bridport Prize. She was also awarded a creative writing fellowship from the National Endowment for the

Arts. Her short stories have appeared in the Connecticut Review, the Chicago Tribune, The Best of Carve Magazine, Short Story Review, Passages North, New Millennium Writings, Cimarron Review, Detroit Noir and others. Her short story collection, Voices of the Lost and Found, won the 2008 National Best Book Award in short fiction. Her website is www.doreneobrien.com.

Drea Jane Kato was born in the great state of California and was raised Buddhist by a gypsy-like artist mother and a Japanese farmer who currently grows pineapples in Hawaii. She is a Capricorn, Dragon, INTJ, HSP, Atheist, singer/songwriter, abstract painter/artist, iPhone photographer who likes yoga, fasting, and the beach. She has been published in magazines such as The Blue Jew Yorker, My Favorite Bullet, Ink Sweat & Tears, The Beat, Ditch, Pomegranate, ReadThis Magazine, Otis Nebula, and Alternativereel.

Drew Pisarra has written a poem for every Fassbinder movie he could find and a few that he couldn't like this one. When not writing poetry, he likes to blog on Korean movies at koreangrindhouse.blogspot.com and tweet on Shakespeare sonnets at @ mistermysterio.

D.S. Jones is a poet from Indiana. His influences range from Bukowski to Tennyson. He has sold poems to Black Heart Magazine and Danse Macabre, An Online Literary Journal. His prose has been published in Bare Back Magazine, Shotgun Honey, and is featured in the Told You So Anthology from Pill Hill Press. Visit thepoetdsjones.com to learn more.

Eamonn Lorigan is an annuated Irishman with a spotty publication history trying to write one decent poem every couple of days for the rest of his miserable God-bedeviled life in the obviously contradictory hope that he will thereby find salvation. Age has not brought him maturity and he tends to be the oldest guy at his local poetry slams. Eamonn's work has appeared in such venues as Carve Magazine, Muse Apprentice Guild, Literary Potpourri, Literary Burlesque, Slowtrains, a Literary Journal, New England Architecture and Poetry Superhighway. He lives in New Hampshire with his wife and two sons.

Ed Makowski is a poet and writer living in Milwaukee, Wisconsin. He prefers cities to suburbs and tents to hotels. Two wheels always trumps four. He is working on his 3rd collection of poetry.

This is **Elena Riley's** first published poem. She's bashful, so instead of telling you more about herself, she's going hide in her room and watch TV.

Ellyn Touchette is a half-crazed biologist from Portland, Maine. She is on the board of directors for Port Veritas, a local poetry reading and nonprofit. Her work is present or forthcoming in The Emerson Review, Ghost House Review, The Open Field, and others. Ellyn plays roller derby, knows what an electrolyte is, and doesn't want to talk about her age.

As a child, **Emily O'Neill** spent most of her time telling mistruths; in some sense, she has always been a storyteller. She studied creative writing at Hampshire College, where her thesis work included a novella about a lake town of hungry ghosts and a poetry collection called Quiet is a Brand of Noise. She recently returned to her beloved New England from an East Coast tour where her poems stretched their legs on stages from Portland to Orlando.

Emily Rose Cole is an emerging poet, folksinger, and MFA-hopeful currently residing in Indianapolis. Her debut solo album, "I Wanna Know," was released in May of 2012. She has forthcoming work in The Eunoia Review, Emerge Literary Journal, and The Rusty Nail.

Emory Bell studies Creative Writing and Physics at Emory University. He watches too much scifi and cannot keep a clean desk.

Eric Roalson lives in Iowa City, Iowa. While his day job keeps food on the table, his real passions are poetry, movies, music, and spiritual philosophy. Phantom kangaroos do exist in his personal universe.

Erin Croy lives in Omaha, NE. She doesn't love talking about herself like this, but thinks you should visit her at www.facebook.com/erinccroy because she wants to talk to people who read poems. Erin has other poems in Origami Condom and Breadcrumb Scabs, and upcoming work in Open Minds Quarterly and The Untidy Season: An Anthology of Nebraska Women's Poetry.

Eryk S. Wenziak is a drummer and teaches management at the graduate level. His poems have appeared or are forthcoming in: elimae; Short, Fast, and Deadly; Thunderclap Press; Used Furniture Review; Negative Suck; Psychic Meatloaf; Dark Chaos; Guerilla Pamphlets; Deadlier Than Thou (anthology); 52 | 250; Long River Run. Currently, he is working on a chapbook, the flowers were trying harder, a collection of prose poems, each accompanied by a photograph.

Faryn Black is a writer from Winnipeg, Canada. In previous incarnations, she has fixed jewellery, wrestled Irish Wolfhounds, and rocked the microphone as a radio announcer. Currently the proud momma to a pack of unruly dogs, she is either a descendant of Sitting Bull, or Leonard Cohen's cousin —depending on what kind of beverage she's drinking. For no discernible reason, cows make her laugh.

Febe Moss hails from the mystical land of Cowboys and big hair. She is a thirty-one year old native Texan, who loves to write about the strange side of life. Currently, she is finishing her first novel and will soon be seeking publication. Febe loves the beat generation, inquiring if the walrus was Paul, and swimming at night. Febe's blog is located at http://thefeebs.blogspot.com/.

Felipe Rivera is co-founder and editor for the La Ventana political journal and its literary supplement, El analfabeto. He has been published in Cipactli, the San Francisco State University Latino art and literature journal, the oldest and longest-lasting of its kind in the United States.

F.J. Bergmann frequents Wisconsin and fibitz.com. She is the poetry editor of Mobius: The Journal of Social Change. She once participated, half-heartedly, in a very small orgy.

Originally from western Pennsylvania, **Francis X. Altomare** currently haunts various pubs between Galway, Ireland and South Florida. He was recently awarded the Oblongata Prize by the Medulla Review for his "City of Lost Things," and his fiction and essays have appeared in various publications, mostly for earthling audiences. When not treating his chronic bibliophilia and avoiding direct sunlight, he teaches Theory, as well as a DIY course on how to take over the world, in South Florida.

Franklin Murdock is a writer and poet from the Midwestern United States. Though most of his work is harvested from the vast landscapes of horror, fantasy, and science fiction, Franklin strives to spin tales outside the conventions of these genres. Beyond fiction, he has written essays that have been published in regional newspapers and that have won contests, has published poetry, has been featured on Internet radio broadcasts, and has written lyrics and music for short films. He also maintains franklinmurdock.com.

Gale Acuff has had poetry published in Ascent, Ohio Journal, Descant, Adirondack Review, Worcester Review, Verse Wisconsin, Maryland Poetry Review, Florida Review, South Carolina Review, Carolina Quarterly, Poem, Amarillo Bay, South Dakota Review, Santa Barbara Review, Sequential Art Narrative in Education, and many other journals. She's authored three books of poetry: Buffalo Nickel (BrickHouse Press, 2004), The Weight of the World (BrickHouse, 2006), and The Story of My Lives (BrickHouse, 2008). He has taught university English in the US, China, and the Palestinian West Bank.

Georgie Delgado is a 21 year old troublemaker from Puerto Rico, who currently resides in Amherst, MA. He loves the moon, Harry Potter books, most sub-genres of metal and punk, Coca-Cola, and Zooey Deschanel. He often wishes that the Universe would reveal that he is, in fact, either a werewolf or a son of Poseidon. In 2009, Georgie was one of five members of Hampshire College's College Nationals poetry slam team, The Human Missile Crisis. That same year, he was awarded Best of the Rest for his poem "Broken Jail Cell Sestina [for john dillinger]." Georgie has one tattoo currently, and a total of 6 planned. The next one he gets will be the Sigil of Cthulhu, as depicted in Lovecraft's "Urilia Text," because Cthulhu is a cool guy as far as ancient evils go, and Georgie likes to imagine that he is too. Cool, that is. Not evil. Maybe ancient, though [there's not much substantial evidence to the contrary, after all].

Glenn W. Cooper lives and writes in Tamworth, Austalia, where he manages an independent bookstore. His books include 'Tryin' To Get To Heaven - Poems About Bob Dylan' and 'His Crucible of Pain: 20 Prose Poems Concerning Rimbaud'. He can be contacted at glennwaynecooper@gmail.com.

Gus Iversen is a native San Franciscan, a founding member of the ILOANBooks literary collective in Brooklyn, NY and the bassist for Phil and the Osophers. He likes cashews, oceans, laundromats, and mechanical pencils. He has a bachelors degree in Creative Writing and consequently works at a veterinary clinic. He was kicked out of Six Flags in New Jersey last summer and briefly banned from the amusement park. This experience informs every aspect of his writing. (www.iloanbooks.com)

Hannah Rose Neuhauser is from Louisville, KY, but currently lives in Ann Arbor where she works at 826michigan. She spends most of her time with words, young authors, and robots. Her work is forthcoming or has recently appeared in Cactus Heart, Maudlin House, and apt. She tweets @velvetraccoon.

Harry Calhoun has been published at odd poetry whistlestops for the past 30 years. Last year, his poems were published in the book The Black Dog and the Road and his chapbooks, Something Real, Near daybreak, with a nod to Frost and Retreating Aggressively into the Dark. He's had recent publications in Chiron Review, Orange Room Review, Gutter Eloquence and many others.

Helen Vitoria's poems can be found and are forthcoming in: elimae, PANK, MudLuscious Press, >kill author, Foundling Review, FRIGG Magazine and Dark Sky Magazine and many others. She is the author of four chapbooks and a full length poetry collection: Corn Exchange is forthcoming from Scrambler Books. Her poems have been nominated for Best New Poets & the Pushcart Prize. She is also an angsty photographer and math and sports make her cry. She is the Founding Editor and Editor in Chief of THRUSH Poetry Journal & THRUSH Press. Find her here: http://helenvitoria-lexis.blogspot.com

Hillary Lyon is founder of and editor for the small poetry house, Subsynchronous Press. Her work has appeared in EOAGH, Shadow Train, Eternal Haunted Summer, Red River Review, and Red Fez, among others. She lives in southern Arizona.

Holly Day has taught writing classes at the Loft Literary Center in Minnesota, since 2000. Her published books include Music Theory for Dummies, Music Composition for Dummies, Guitar All-in-One for Dummies, Piano All-in-One for Dummies, Walking Twin Cities, Insider's Guide to the Twin Cities, Nordeast Minneapolis: A History, and The Book Of, while her poetry has recently appeared in Oyez Review, SLAB, and Gargoyle. Her newest poetry book, Ugly Girl, just came out from Shoe Music Press.

Howie Good, a journalism professor at SUNY New Paltz, is the author of the full-length poetry collections Lovesick (Press Americana, 2009), Heart With a Dirty Windshield (BeWrite Books, 2010), and Everything Reminds Me of Me (Desperanto, 2011), as well as numerous print and digital chapbooks.

Israel Wasserstein's poetry and prose have appeared in Crab Orchard Review, Flint Hills Review, Coal City Review, and elsewhere. His first poetry collection, This Ecstasy They Call Damnation, was a 2013 Kansas Notable Book.

Jack Hodil is an English major and Creative Writing minor at the University of Richmond. His poems have been published in a handful of magazines, such as Word Riot and the Camroc Press Review. He finds his hands too dangerous and his feet misleading.

Jackson Burgess is a writer, painter, and student at the University of Southern California. His work has been published in various American and Australian magazines, including The Storyteller, Stepping Stones Magazine: ALMIA, and SpeedPoets Zine. You can find him longboarding barefoot, watching clouds, or crying himself to sleep around South Central LA. To see his full publishing history or to make sure he's still alive, check out his personal blog: jacksonburgess.wordpress.com.

Jacob Luplow grew up in Seattle, Washington. He is a current student at Cornell College, a writer and photographer, and he is currently working on a collection of poems titled "Like Lotus Through Glass" and a body of art titled "Di-Methyl Tryptamine." His art has been featured in Subliminal Interiors.

James Dowell lives in Frisco, Texas. He has a Bachelor's degree in Electronics Engineering he does not use. He loves devil's food, looking at the stars, his wife Michelle and his son Arden, reading the Bible, and the romantic poets, Moby Dick & Phantasms of the Living... and like all true poets, listening to the wind, needless to say not in that order. He has several blogs in development on the web and a particular obsession with Fortean topics. He believes in God and aliens. He really did run away and join the circus once upon a time.

Janann Dawkins' work has appeared in publications such as decomP, Existere, Mezzo Cammin, Ouroboros Review & Two Review, among others. Leadfoot Press published her chapbook Micropleasure in 2008. A graduate of Grinnell College with a B.A. in American Studies & twice nominated for the Pushcart Prize, she resides in Ann Arbor, MI.

Jane Røken believes in coloured lanterns and old tractors. She has been a saxhorn player in a brass band, a research technician in a secret lab, and a member of the Fourth International. Now past sixty, she has not yet decided what she wants to be when she grows up. In the meantime, she writes weird stories and spooky poems. For you. Yes, you.

Jason Brightwell lives in Baltimore, Md. He is regularly haunted by one thing or another, and is always searching for the right thing to say. His work has appeared in journals including The Blind Man's Rainbow and will be included in an upcoming issue of The Battered Suitcase. You can find him blathering on and on at www. blatheranddrone.blogspot.com.

Jay Coral thinks he knows where the ducks in the pond go during the winter. Ask him, he dares you to ask him. He blogs occcassionally at http://bluejayeye.blogspot.com/.

Jean Brasseur lives in Northern Virginia with her husband, two children, two dogs, six ferrets and other assorted pets. When not working or cleaning up after the aforementioned roomies, she enjoys all types of poetry particularly that written by new and unknown poets. Jean has been writing poetry for as long as she can remember, but only became serious about her craft a few years ago when impending birthdays made her realize it was now or never. Since then her work has appeared in The Battered Suitcase, gutter eloquence,twenty20, the right eyed deer and others.

Jeanie Tomasko is the author of two books of poetry, Sharp as Want (Little Eagle Press) and Tricks of Light (Parallel Press.) She lives in Wisconsin where all kinds of creepy things happen.

Jeannine Geise is the rare, contented high school English teacher. She graduated with her MFA in Creative Writing this past summer from Ashland University, and currently resides near Dayton, Ohio with her handsome husband, Colin; her impressive collection of X-Men comic books; and her two cats, Socrates and Kittah. (Notice the impressive use of semicolons!) To read more about Jeannine and her work, visit her at: http://www.jeanninegeise.wordpress.com/

Jeffrey Park's poetry has appeared most recently in unFold, Aberration Labyrinth, Burningword, and the science fiction anthology Just One More Step from Horrified Press. A native of Baltimore, Jeffrey currently lives in Munich, Germany, where he works at a private secondary school. Links to all of his published work can be found at www. scribbles-and-dribbles.com.

Jennifer Lobaugh is a writer, musician, and current student at the University of Oklahoma. Fluent in English, French, Russian, and Sarcasm, her poetry has recently been published at The Camel Saloon and is forthcoming in Gutter Eloquence Magazine. She's pretty sure a ghost once kidnapped her pet turtle.

Jennifer Phillips is a MFA candidate in poetry at Minnesota State University at Moorhead. She has worked in biomedical sciences and knows way too much about how creepy biology can be.

Jennifer L. Tomaloff (b. 1972) | author, bending light into verse (put it down) | takes: pictures | likes: animals | hates: people | see: bendinglightintoverse.com

Jeston Dulin is a graduate of Northwest Missouri State University's M.A. English program, and currently teaches composition there. His flash fiction piece, "Prodigal Son" is forthcoming in the May 2014 issue of "Apocrypha and Abstractions." Jeston's writing revolves around themes of nostalgia and a questioning of reality.

Jill Khoury earned her MFA from The Ohio State University. Her poems have appeared or are forthcoming in numerous journals, including Blood Lotus, RHINO, and Inter|rupture. She has been nominated for two Pushcart Prizes and a Best of the Net award. Her chapbook Borrowed Bodies was released from Pudding House Press. You can find her at jillkhoury.com.

Jim Bronyaur lives in Pennsylvania and has been published in many anthologies including End of Days (Volume 4), Were-What?, and Creepy Things. Other stories have been published with Flashes in the Dark, House of Horrors, Pow! Fast Flash Fiction, Twisted Tongue, and many others. He doesn't sleep, drinks lots of coffee, and listens to Guns 'n Roses. Jim's web site is www.JimBronyaur.com. Better yet, follow Jim on Twitter - @jimbronyaur.

Jim Davis is a graduate of Knox College and now lives, writes, and paints in Chicago. Jim edits the North Chicago Review, and his work has appeared in After Hours, Blue Mesa Review, Poetry Quarterly, The Ante Review, Chiron Review, andContemporary American Voices, among others. Jim will see two of his collections go to print in 2012: Lead, then Gold(unbound content) and Elements of Course: Crafty Abstraction (MiTe Press) www.jimdavispoetry.com.

Jim Eigo has written on theater, dance, art, literature, sex and the design of clinical trials. He helped design two reforms of AIDS drug regulation, accelerated approval and expanded access, reforms that facilitated the delivery of many treatments to people across the world. His short fiction has appeared in such volumes as Best American Gay Fiction #3, in such periodicals as The Chicago Review and at such online venues as Cleaver Magazine and Bohemia. His first published art work appears in The Poetics of Space from Intima Press.

Joan McNerney's poetry has been included in numerous literary magazines such as Seven Circle Press, Dinner with the Muse, Blueline, Spectrum, three Bright Spring Press Anthologies and several Kind of A Hurricane Publications. She has been nominated three times for Best of the Net. Poet and Geek recognized her work as their best poem of 2013. Four of her books have been published by fine small literary presses and she has three e-book titles.

Joe Love is an artist, a musician, and a poet and teaches writing and literature in St. Louis on both sides of the arch. His work has appeared in or is forthcoming from The Oddville Press, Crack the Spine, Bangalore Review, From the Depths, Drunk Monkeys, Bellowing Ark, and other journals.

Joe Nicholas is an experimenter and experiencer who enjoys wine, felines, broccoli, puns, and all things bizarre. He has work published or forthcoming in Willard & Maple, Dead Flowers, Sugared Water, Star*Line, and various haiku journals.

John Grey is an Australian born poet, works as financial systems analyst. Recently published in Poem, Caveat Lector, Prism International and the horror anthology, "What Fears Become" with work upcoming in Big Muddy, Prism International and Pinyon.

John Joe Loftus originally started out in life as an alternate persona, but has since taken complete control of the biological unit. He has a growing interest in poetic composition and has recently acquired a taste for strong drink and women. He shows no sign of relinquishing control of the unit, formerly a student of marine chemistry at NUIG as well as a highly accomplished tree-feller in a misguided desert nation. His hobbies included cookery, hiking and the ruthless enforcement of his will. He is dearly missed by his family and friends.

John Roth is a native Ohioan who haunts his parent's basement. His poems have appeared in Red Fez, Red River Review, and The Red Booth Review. He likes the color red; scandalous red.

John Swain lives in Louisville, Kentucky. His fifth chapbook, Handing the Cask, recently appeared from erbacce press.

Joseph Harms is the author of the novels Baal and Cant. His fiction and poetry have appeared in Boulevard, The Alaskan Quarterly Review, IthacaLit, Out of Our, Poydras Review, Red Ochre Press, Lines+Stars, Bad Idea, SPECS, Mad Hatters' Review, The American Dissident, Mandala Journal, Niche, Wilderness House Literary Review, Otis Nebula, The Olive Tree Review and, among others, Poetry Pacific. He is currently seeking a publisher for his sonnet series Bel.

Joseph M. Gant is a scientific glassblower by trade but a writer by passion. His work has appeared modestly in the independent, academic, and commercial press. Joseph lives in the Philadelphia area where he edits poetry for Sex and Murder Magazine. His first full-length collection of poetry, Zero Division, is forthcoming with Rebel Satori Press.

Joshua Otto is an itinerant who's interested in the reflections of teams, and new translations of Spanish-American poetry as forms of extreme patriotism. He currently lives with ducks in North Portland, Oregon.

Jude Cowan is a writer, artist and composer who lives in London. She works as an archivist for Reuters Television. Her first collection of poetry, For the Messengers was published by Donut Press in 2011. Her second, The Groodoyals of Terre Rouge will be published by Dark Windows Press in 2012. She makes musical improvisations on Reuters stories and these are available on the Parisian based netlabel Three Legs Duck.

Julia Rox is a poet from Nashville, TN. She is a senior at Lipscomb University, studying English: Writing and Philosophy. Her work explores themes of creation and destruction--the creation and destruction we engage in with language as well as the creation and destruction we engage in daily with ourselves and our identity. Her work has been published in On the Cusp Zine, Fractal Magazine, and the Lipscomb College of Arts and Sciences Magazine.

Justin Holliday teaches English. His poetry has been featured in Glitterwolf, Sanitarium, Leaves of Ink, and elsewhere. His reviews has been featured in New Orleans Review, Lehigh Valley Vanguard, and The Adroit Journal.

Kalen Rowe is a kid in Houston, Texas. He has lived in Idaho, Montana, California, and Colorado. He has been published by Gargoyle Magazine, The Aletheia, and few times by Glass Mountain. In 2013, he helped found and now assists with Anklebiters Publishing, which prints Poets Anonymous and Mimic Magazine. kalenrowe.com.

Kara Synhorst is a lifelong Sacramentan who has never lived more than seven miles from her childhood home. She got her B.A., teaching credential, and M.F.A. from CSU Sacramento and now teaches English at Luther Burbank High. She lives with her husband Reza and daughter Azadeh and two ornery cats. Her poems have appeared in Poetry Now, Convergence, The Found Poetry Review, unFold, and Susurrus.

Kate Frank is a fifth generation Oregonian going to school in Western Massachusetts, where she co-hosts a weekly poetry open mic and slam. Her work has appeared in The Reader and on various stages from Maine to Minnesota. She believes in Buffy the Vampire Slayer, brunch and beer.

Kayla Bashe is a writer/actress studying at Sarah Lawrence. Her work has appeared in Vitality Magazine, Liminality Magazine, and The Future Fire, and her suspense/magical realism/subversive romance novellas are available from Torquere Press and Less Than Three Press.

Keith Higginbotham's poetry has appeared recently or is forthcoming in The Beatnik, Cricket Online Review, ditch, Eratio, The Montucky Review, and Otoliths. He is the author of Carrying the Air on a Stick (The Runaway Spoon Press), Prosaic Suburban Commercial (Eratio Editions), and Theme From Next Date (Ten Pages Press).

Kevin Heaton writes in South Carolina. His latest chapbook, "Measured Days," has published at Heavy Hands Ink Press. His work has appeared in: Elimae, Nibble, The Catalonian Review, Bananafish Magazine, and many others. His is listed as a notable poet at: KansasPoets.com. More of his work can be seen at: http://kevinheatonpoetry.webstarts.com/publications.html

Kevin Ridgeway is a writer from Southern California, where he dwells in a shady bungalow with his girlfriend and a one-eyed cat. Sometimes he and the cat engage in staring contests. Recent work has appeared in Underground Voices, Red Fez, The Camel Saloon, Haggard & Halloo and Magic Cat Press.

KG Newman is the editor of a high school sports website, ColoradoSportsNetwork. com, and lives in Aurora, Colo. He is an Arizona State University graduate and his first collection of poems, While Dreaming of Diamonds in Wintertime, is available on Amazon.

Khadija Hussain is currently a junior at an arts high school, where she studies poetry closely under the guidance of poet Bruce Cohen. She has been published in Bard College's Yolk Magazine, and Sunken Garden Poetry's online magazine, Theodate. She has also been awarded prizes on a national level by the Scholastic Art and Writing recognition program.

Khalym Kari Burke-Thomas beats dead sticks with horses. His work appears in New Wave Vomit, DOGZPLOT, and amphibi.us. He is majoring in Asian Languages and Cultures at Hobart and William Smith Colleges, where he also serves as Assistant to the Director of the Trias Residency for Writers. He "blogs" over at Moon Prism Power.

Kimberly Casey is a Massachusetts poet who has made her home in every corner of the state. An Emerson College graduate and member of Emerson's 2010 College Unions Poetry Slam Invitational team, Kimberly remains active in the poetry scene both in Boston and Worcester, while nesting in her current town of Westfield, where she can be spotted constantly sipping tea, writing, and dreaming.

Kirby Wright was born and raised in Honolulu, Hawaii. He is a graduate of Punahou School in Honolulu and the University of California at San Diego. He received his MFA in Creative Writing from San Francisco State University. Wright has been nominated for two Pushcart Prizes and is a past recipient of the Ann Fields Poetry Prize, the Academy of American Poets Award, the Browning Society Award for Dramatic Monologue, and Arts Council Silicon Valley Fellowships in Poetry and The Novel. BEFORE THE CITY, his first book of poetry, took First Place at the 2003 San Diego Book Awards.

KJ likes to make poems a lot. Find his work in Thieves Jargon, decomp, and gutter eloquence.

Kristin Maffei is a poet and copywriter living in New York City. She was educated at Sarah Lawrence College and the University of Oxford, and holds an MFA from New York University where she was a Goldwater Fellow in Poetry and co-curator of the NYU Emerging Writers Series at KGB Bar. She is a copywriter at Oxford University Press and co-founder of the collaborative literary 'zine Call & Response.

Kyla Cheung is a student at Columbia University. She works in languages, prose, and code, and aspires to be the text big thing.

Kyle Hemmings lives and works in New Jersey. He has been published in Elimae, Smokelong Quarterly, This Zine Will Change Your Life, Blaze Vox, Matchbook, and elsewhere. He loves 50s Sci-Fi movies, manga comics, and pre-punk garage bands of the 60s. He blogs at http://upatberggasse19.blogspot.com/

Laura Grodin is a recent graduate of Adelphi University's Creative Writing MFA program. Laura is a recipient of the Donn Axinn Award in short fiction, and her work can be seen in Postcard Shorts and Milk Sugar Literature. Laura is a California native who now resides in Brooklyn, New York.

Laura Hardy was born and raised in the Santa Cruz Mountains. She writes scripts & poetry as a hobby, which has never led to publishing, only the completion of three chapbooks: L'Amour, Notes, and I Won't Lie Anymore. Much of her inspiration for character comes from Tommy Wiseau.

Laura LeHew is the author of a full-length book of poems, two chapbooks, numerous articles and with poems in Anobium, American Society: What Poet's See, Collecting Life: Poets on Objects Known and Imagined, Eleven Eleven, PANK and Phantom Kangaroo among others. She is on the steering committee for the Lane Literary Guild and is an active volunteer for the Oregon Poetry Association having held a variety of positions including President and Contest Chair. Laura interned for, and is a former board member, of CALYX Press. She received her MFA from the California College of Arts. She writes, edits her small press Uttered Chaos www.utteredchaos.org and sharpens her claws in Eugene, Oregon.

Lauren D.M. Smith is a Canadian currently living and working in Japan as an ALT (assistant language teacher). She is a recent graduate from Bishop's University and is currently trying to find a job back home to support her writing habit.

In 1983, **Lawrence Gladeview** was born to two proud and semi-doting parents. After two middle schools and losing his faith in catholic high school, he graduated from James Madison University, majoring in English and having spent only one night in jail. He is a Boulder, Colorado poet cohabiting with his fiance Rebecca Barkley. Lawrence is one of two editors for MediaVirus Magazine, and more than sixty of his poems have been featured, or are forthcoming in various print and online publications. You can read more of his poetry on his website, Righteous Rightings.

Lee Gillespie despite being both an advocate and an avatar for the trickster god Coyote somehow ended up as a mother of 2 and being owned by a black cat that hates her socks. When she was young she wanted to be just like Lord Byron -"Mad, bad, and dangerous to know." Unfortunately, she failed to notice that unlike her, Byron did take the occasional break from general debauchery to actually publish something.

Usually something better than what she could up with. She's hoping to make up some lost time now or at least make up something interesting now and again.

Leila A. Fortier is a writer, artist, poet, and photographer currently residing on the remote island of Okinawa Japan. Her rich interplay of mediums from macro photography, to oils, acrylics, water colors, pastels, and digital techniques, are then layered and arranged to invoke the viewer into raw, emotional experience. Her restlessness is expressed in her passion to make manifest the formless in what she calls Painting Emotion. Her work has been featured in tandem with her poetic works, published in numerous literary magazines, journals, and reviews both in print and online. She has been selected to appear as the cover or featured artist of many virtual galleries and publications including Diverse Voices Quarterly, Cave Moon Press, and Pink Panther Magazine to name a few. A complete listing of all her works can be found at: www.leilafortier.com.

Levi Gribbon's work has appeared in Blinking Cursor Literary Magazine, Blink Ink, and Hobo Pancakes. He is a creative writing student at Concordia University St. Paul.

Linda Crate is a Pennsylvanian native born in Pittsburgh yet raised in the rural town of Conneautville. Her poetry has been published in various journals the latest of which include: Skive, Speech Therapy, The Scarlet Sound, Itasca Illinois Poetry & Willow Tree Dreams, Dead Snakes, and Carnage Conservatory.

Lisa Marie Basile is the author of the forthcoming A Decent Voodoo, (Cervená Barva Press, 2012) and a chapbook, Diorama (Wisp Press). She recently was published in Pear Noir!, >kill author, Foundling Review and Moon Milk Review. She is the founding editor and publisher of Patasola Press and currently reads poetry for Weave Magazine. She performs with the Poetry Brothel as Luna Liprari and is an M.F.A. candidate at The New School. She is a member of the Poetry Society of New York.

Lisa M. Litrenta is a 22-year-old New Englander who tries to live her life compassionately. Follow her on twitter.com/lisamlitrenta.

Lisa McCool-Grime loves Sappho, collaborations and wallflower women. Her publications include Splinter Generation. Her collaborative work with Nancy Flynn can be read at Poemeleon. Tupelo press awarded one of her Sappho-inspired poems first place in their Fragments of Sappho contest.

Lori Lamothe has published two poetry collections, Happily and Trace Elements, as well as a few chapbooks, most recently Ouija in Suburbia with dancing girl press. She lives in New England with her daughter and a Siberian husky born on Halloween.

Lucia Olga Ahrensdorf is sixteen years old. She enjoys fencing in sketchy warehouses and writing poetry while she procrastinates for physics labs.

Luis Cuauhtemoc Berriozabal lives in Southern California. He works in the mental health field. His poetry and prose has appeared in online and print journals. His chapbook, Songs For Oblivion, will appear later this year from Alternating Current Press.

Maggie Armstrong has been a Siamese twin, a murderer, a cuckold, and a loaf of bread. She has been all of these things and none of these things. She is a liar. She is a zombie. She is uncomfortable with the concept of tuna fish from a can. She cannot tell time or blow up a balloon. She does not want to go to bed. Ever. She wants to sleep forever. She is you and you are she.

Louisiana girl **Margaret Emma Brandl** once studied abroad in Japan and hasn't stopped talking about it since. A graduate of the University of Alabama, she recently won the Michael Goodson Award for Poetry and will be starting an MFA in creative writing at Notre Dame in the fall.

Marina Rubin's first chapbook Ode to Hotels came out in 2002, followed by Once in 2004 and Logic in 2007. Her work had appeared in hundreds of magazines including 13th Warrior Review, Asheville Poetry Review, Dos Passos Review, 5AM, Nano Fiction, Coal City, Green Hills Literary Lantern, Jewish Currents, Lillith, Pearl, Poet Lore, Skidrow Penthouse, The Portland Review, The Worcester Review and many more. She is an associate editor of Mudfish. She has been nominated for the Pushcart. She lives in New York where she works as a headhunter on Wall Street while writing her fourth book, a collection of flash fiction stories.

Margaret Mary is named after St. Margaret Mary of the Sacred Heart of Jesus, and was told it was sinful to shorten her name. Unfortunately, she shortens it daily. She started writing poetry when she was homeless, as a way to pass the time. No longer homeless, she is learning jiujitsu and kickboxing in case of a zombie invasion, while finishing her degree in political science. Margaret Mary's poetry tends to be dark, absurd with a half narrative, and sometimes political but mostly not so much. Was it mentioned that she likes puns?

Mark Bonica is a father, husband, soldier, photographer, and oddly, economics professor. His poetry has appeared in a variety of online and print magazines including Words-Myth, Righthandpointing, Oak Bend Review, and others. He has recently published a chap book, Oneironaut, and a collection of short fiction, Love Stories in Extraordinary Time. He blogs at recalcitrantegg.blogspot.com, and www.bonicaphoto.com/blog.

Mary Elzabeth Lee lives in Red Lion, PA. She attends Penn State York where she is the co-editor of Any Other Word. Her poems have appeared in Parody Magazine, The Golden Key, and Bellow Magazine.

Matt Ryan is the author of Read This Or You're Dead To Me:(forthcoming from

Hopewell Publications). His work has appeared in numerous journals, including Pindeldyboz, Word Riot, Mud Luscious, Ghoti and Opium. He is the publisher and editor of the poetry press, Lowbrow Press, the fiction editor of Best New Writing and teaches creative and academic writing at Concordia St. Paul University.

Matt Schumacher's poetry chapbook of fantastical drinking songs, favorite maritime drinking songs of the miraculous alcoholics, was published last year, and his third book of poetry, Ghost Town Odes, will be published in 2016. He helps edit Phantom Drift and lives in Portland, Oregon.

By day, **Matthew Specht** is the Harbormaster of Reefpoint Marina in Racine, WI. By night, he is tired, and cuddles with a local chupacabra of some repute.. www. jumpymatt.com.

Matthew Byrne is an insurance broker in Chicago. His poetry appears in some journals, most notably Best American Poetry 2007. He is married and has 3 children. He is addicted to hot sauce, practices yoga, and harbors an (irrational?) aversion to U2 and Dave Matthews.

When eight years old, **Matthew Harrison** was shunned at daycare for trying to hold séances in a bathroom. Now he lives in Massachusetts. He watches too many monster movies, takes long night walks, writes about spooks and creatures, and he still hasn't seen a ghost.

Meaghan Ford was born a witch but lost all of her magic in an a card game at the Cantab Lounge on poetry night. This led to a paradox in the universe causing people to misspell her name for the rest of her life. This year she received her Masters in Creative Writing, Nonfiction from Emerson College and officially declared herself an ardent liar. She's been recently published in both The Legendary and The Scrambler and aspires to one day be Queen of the Emerald Necklace in Boston, Massachusetts.

Megan Kennedy has been forging dark art for over ten years, and hopes one day it will make her an oracle. Her work has been featured in SNAP! and Vicious Magazine, Fantastic Horror Magazine, as the cover art for numerous local and international bands, as well as an upcoming release from Random House Australia.

Melanie Browne likes to eat crispy creme donuts while watching the third class steerage dance scene from the movie Titanic over and over again. She also has an online literary journal that you should check out: http://theliteraryburlesque.com/.

Melissa Bobe holds an MFA in Creative Writing and Literary Translation from Queens College of the City University of New York. In the spring of 2011, she was a writer-in-residence at the Louis Armstrong House Museum Archives. She founded and taught a creative writing workshop for teens at the Rockville Centre Public Library for six years, and has also taught nonfiction prose writing as an adjunct instructor at Queens College. She is currently pursuing a PhD in English Literature at Rutgers University.

Meredith Weiers graduated from Carnegie Mellon University and lives in southern Maryland.

Michael Andrew is a full time student at NUIG studying Philosophy and Celtic Civilisation. His work has appeared in Blue and yellow dog, shamrock, mancini press, guerilla pamphlets et.al. He can be found here: http://www.facebook.com/profile.php?id=622160272 . Or alternatively you can visit him for a cup of tea in Galway.

Michael Bagwell lives and writes in West Chester, Pennsylvania. His work has recently appeared or is forthcoming in Dark Sky Magazine, Breadcrumb Scabs, Short, Fast and Deadly, and Collective Fallout, among others.

Michael Dwayne Smith's most recent collection, "What the Weather's Like, Only Stranger", arrives spring 2014 from Emerge/EIJ Publications. Post-hippie professor, editor in chief at Mojave River Press & Review, he's been awarded both the Hinderaker Prize for poetry and the Polonsky Prize for fiction. His work appears in excellent journals like burntdistrict, Word Riot, Stone Highway Review, decomP, >kill author, and the Cortland Review. He lives near a ghost town in the Mojave Desert with his wife and rescued animals.

Michael Frissore has a chapbook called Poetry is Dead (Coatlism, 2009) and a blog called michaelfrissore.blogspot.com. His writing has been nominated for the Pushcart Prize and Dzanc Books' "Best of the Web" series, and included in humor anthologies alongside the likes of Sarah Silverman and Patton Oswalt. He grew up in Massachusetts and lives in Oro Valley, Arizona with his wife and son.

Michael Grover is a poet, originally from Florida, who has lived in L.A. and Philadelphia. He now lives in Toledo, Ohio in a notoriously haunted building where he writes, publishes, and prints chapbooks. Michael is the head poetry editor at www.redfez.net.

Michael H. Brownstein has been widely published throughout the small and literary presses. His work has appeared in The Café Review, American Letters and Commentary, Skidrow Penthouse, Xavier Review, Hotel Amerika, Free Lunch, Meridian Anthology of Contemporary Poetry, The Pacific Review, Poetrysuperhighway.com and others. In addition, he has nine poetry chapbooks including The Shooting Gallery (Samidat Press, 1987), Poems from the Body Bag (Ommation Press, 1988), A Period of Trees (Snark Press, 2004), What Stone Is (Fractal Edge Press, 2005), I Was a Teacher Once (Ten Page Press, 2011) and Firestorm: A Rendering of Torah (Camel Saloon Press, 2012). He is the editor of First Poems from Viet Nam(2011). Brownstein taught elementary school in Chicago's inner city (he is now retired), but he continues to study authentic African instruments, conducts grant-writing workshops for educators, designs websites and records performance and music pieces with grants from the City of Chicago's Department of Cultural Affairs, the Oppenheimer Foundation, BP Leadership Grants, and others.

Michael Keenan received his MFA in Literary Arts from Brown University. His first chapbook, "Two Girls," was published by Say No Press in 2009, and his first book, "Translations On Waking In An Italian Cemetery," will be released by A-Minor Press in 2014. His writing has appeared in Fence, Alice Blue Review, Shampoo, Paul Revere's Horse, and Arsenic Lobster, among others, and is forthcoming in Poetry International.

Michael Kriesel, 50, is a poet and reviewer whose work has appeared in Alaska Quarterly, Antioch Review, Crab Creek Review, Rattle, Small Press Review, Library Journal, Nimrod, North American Review, Rosebud, and the Progressive. He served on the Wisconsin Poet Laureate Commission from 2006-2008, and won the 2011 Wisconsin People & Ideas Poetry Contest, the 2009 Wisconsin Fellowship Of Poets Muse Prize, and the 2004 Lorine Niedecker Poetry Prize from the Council for Wisconsin Writers. He was featured poet for the 2010 Great Lakes Writers Festival. Books include Chasing Saturday Night: Poems About Rural Wisconsin (Marsh River Editions) and Moths Mail the House (Sunnyoutside). He's also the Wisconsin Fellowship of Poets Conference Coordinator. He has a B.S. in Literature from the University of the State of New York, and was a print and broadcast journalist in the U.S. Navy from 1980-1990. He's currently a janitor at the rural elementary school he once attended.

Midori Chen is a writer from San Francisco. She likes to bear witness to the little things— a new nest on an old branch, a half-buried uncut key. She likes her poetry to sustain those small moments.

Mike Salgado is a poet and Training Senior Specialist with Eurofins Lancaster Labs. He is also a poetry and art editor for Marathon Literary Review. You can find more of Mike's work in Third Point Press, Lehigh Valley Vanguard, and G3: Genes, Genomes, Genomics. He has poetry forthcoming in The Electronic Encyclopedia of Experimental Literature by tNY.Press. Mike currently resides in Lancaster, PA where he is active in the growing literary community. Find him online at Michael Salgado Poetry & Further.

Mike Meraz is a poet from Los Angeles who currently lives in New Orleans. He is the author of two books of poetry, Black-Listed Poems and All Beautiful Things Travel Alone. Both are available at Lulu.com and Amazon.com. He is also the editor of Black-Listed Magazine.

M. J. Luppa lives on a small farm near the shores of Lake Ontario. Her most recent poems have appeared in Poetry East, The Chariton Review, Tar River Poetry, Blueline, The Prose Poem Project, and The Centrifugal Eye, among other publications. Her most recent poetry chapbook is As the Crow Flies (Foothills Publishing, 2008), and her second full-length collection is Within Reach (Cherry Grove Collections, 2010).

Between Worlds, a prose chapbook, was published by Foothills Publishing in May 2013. She is Writer-in-Residence and Director of the Visual and Performing Arts Minor program at St. John Fisher College in Rochester, New York.

M. Krochmalnik Grabois' poems have appeared in hundreds of literary magazines in the U.S. and abroad. He is a regular contributor to The Prague Revue, and has been nominated for the Pushcart Prize, most recently for his story "Purple Heart" published in The Examined Life in 2012, and for his poem. "Birds," published in The Blue Hour, 2013. His novel, Two-Headed Dog, based on his work as a clinical psychologist in a state hospital, is available for 99 cents from Kindle and Nook, or as a print edition.

Molly Hamilton is a writer who is inspired by myths and legends. She enjoys writing stories that allow readers to discover new creatures and new explanations. Her goal, as a writer, is to entertain all who are bored and cheer all who are lonely with her writing. When Molly is not hanging out with her story characters, she is usually with her family or attending college.

Molly Kat is currently living in an intentional community in the mountains of North Carolina. She likes to grow her own food, challenge her mind, dissect words, and propagate madness. She is obsessed with the idea of viewing collapse in a deconstructed way so that its positive potential can be realized and implemented. Molly gives really great hugs and likes to spend her time working with children. She has been published in print and online, and writes for the popular blog http://selfiesinink.com.

Monica Rico is obsessed with the Saturn V rocket, Japanese knives, and the proper cooking of eggs. She has an M.A. in Creative Writing from CCNY and spends most of her time editing a literary journal, working around the food industry, and reading.

Mora Torres' work has been published in The Pony Express, Cul-de-sac, Fortunates, Emerge and many, many bathroom stalls. She lives in Los Angeles, drinks lattes and scowls at the passersby. This sustains her.

Morgan Adams grew up in a small used bookstore in Lexington, Kentucky. To this day, she cannot pass by a disorderly bookshelf without attempting to straighten it. Her work has been published in Carillon: A Journal of Writing and Art and featured on The Poet's Weave podcast

Nancy Flynn grew up on the Susquehanna River in northeastern Pennsylvania, spent many years on a downtown creek in Ithaca, New York, and now lives near the mighty Columbia in Portland, Oregon. She attended Oberlin College, Cornell University, and has an M.A. in English from SUNY at Binghamton. Her writing has received an Oregon Literary Fellowship and the James Jones First Novel Fellowship. Her poetry collection, Every Door Recklessly Ajar, was published in 2015; her long poem, "Great Hunger" will appear as an Anchor & Plume pocket book in early 2016. Her website is www. nancyflynn.com.

Nazifa Islam is a poet from Novi, Michigan. She has the misfortune of being born on the day that resulted in Abraham Lincoln's assassination as well as the sinking of the Titanic. As if in accord with these ominous tidings, her favorite poets are Sylvia Plath, Dorothy Parker, Dorothea Lasky and Edgar Allan Poe. She has work forthcoming in both Breadcrumb Scabs and Disingenuous Twaddle, and regularly updates her blog Thoughts Interjected.

Natalie Angelone is an English major and writing and communication minor at Concordia University St. Paul, MN.

Nate maxson is a 24-year-old poet and performance artist from Albuquerque, New Mexico.

Nathan Lipps spent his childhood in the fields and forests along the coast of Lake Michigan. He is currently an MFA student at Wichita State University, where he also teaches.

Nathan Logan is the author of the chapbooks Arby's Combo Roundup (Mondo Bummer), Dick (Pangur Ban Party), and Holly from Muncie (Spooky Girlfriend Press). He is a doctoral student in creative writing at the University of North Texas.

Nathan Savin Scott has lived in Boston, New Orleans, San Francisco, and now lives in our nation's capital. He doesn't know a thing about politics and thus usually sits awkwardly and silent during dinner parties he attends there. His work has appeared in some online magazines and some print ones, as well. You can find him on Twitter: @ nathan_s_scott.

Neil Ellman lives and writes in New Jersey, but his poetry, including five chapbooks of ekphrastic works, appears throughout the world. For more details, he can be Googled, but please note that he is not the Neil Ellman who is the accountant, professional arm wrestler, or drag queen. He is the other one.

Neil Weston is from the UK. He has micro fiction, flash fiction published and due to be published at Cuento Magazine, Infective Ink, The Eschatology Journal, Diamond Point Press-twenty20journal and Folded Word: PIC FIC.

Nic Alea is sometimes socially awkward/sometimes poet/sometimes queer person/ sometimes practicer of magic/sometimes lover/sometimes san francisco dweller/ sometimes sagittarius/sometimes artist/but mostly all of the time.

Nicole Taylor has many hopeful projects, no MFA's and is an artist, a hiker, a volunteer and a dancer, formerly in DanceAbility. She blogs at www.

apoetessanthology.blogspot.com/, www.facebook.com/Pushk1n, and www.oregonpoeticvoices.org/.

Nico Rico is a Lansing, Michigan based photographer. She received her AAS in Photographic Imaging in 2015. Her work has been featured on Slurpee All Access Chill, Tight Blue Jeans, City Pulse, Revue West Michigan, and New Noise Magazine. She shoots events, concerts, fashion, fine art, promotional and commercial photography.

P.A.Levy, having fled his native East End, now hides in the heart of Suffolk countryside learning the lost arts of hedge mumbling and clod watching. He has been published in many magazines, and is an original member of the Clueless Collective to be found at: www.cluelesscollective.co.uk.

Paula Chew is a writer living in New York. She wheedles her time away writing poetry, criticism, and personal essays about ghosts (and sometimes other topics). You can read her work here and keep up with her inane thoughts here.

Paul Hellweg has had over one hundred poems published since his debut in 2009. He won the 2009 Coatlism Press full-length poetry book contest, and he has been nominated for a Pushcart Prize. Alas, he has nothing scandalous to confess, but he thinks that's a grand idea and he promises to do something scandalous as soon as inspiration strikes.

Paul m. Strohm is a freelance journalist working in Houston, Texas. He cataloged the unpublished correspondence of D.H. Lawrence while working at the Humanities Research Center at UT-Austin. Even the famous begin letters with 'Dear * * * * * *, I am fine. How are you?" His most recent collection of poems was published by the Wellhead Press in 2013.

Paul McQuade was born in Glasgow, Scotland, but now lives in Tokyo where he reads, writes and teaches. Occasionally he survives earthquakes. His work has most recently appeared in Goblin Fruit, Fractured West and Six Sentences. He has a tattoo of a teacup on his left arm and a penchant for Hendrick's gin.

Peter Marra is from Williamsburg Brooklyn. Born in Brooklyn, he lived in the East Village, New York from 1979-1987 at the height of the punk – no wave rebellion. His poems explore alienation, sex, love, addiction, the havoc that secrets can wreak and obsessions often recounted in an oneiric filmic haze. He wishes to find new methods of description and language manipulation wrapped in a frenzy. He has either been published in or has work forthcoming in Caper Literary Journal, amphibi.us, Yes Poetry, Maintenant 4 & 5, Beatnik, Crash, Danse Macabre, Clutching At Straws, O Sweet Flowery Roses, Breadcrumb Scabs, Carcinogenic,Carnage Conservatory,Subliminal Interiors,and Calliope Nerve among others. He was recently interviewed by Yes, Poetry and is currently constructing his first collection of poems.

Peter Schwartz's poetry has been featured in The Collagist, The Columbia Review, Diagram, and Opium Magazine. His latest collection Old Men, Girls, and Monsters was published as part of the Achilles Chapbook Series. He's an interviewer for the PRATE Interview Series, a regular contributor to The Nervous Breakdown, and the art editor for DOGZPLOT.

Peter Taylor appears in Australia, Canada, Romania, the United Kingdom, and the United States. His poems explore how history shapes our perceptions of the world. Trainer and The Masons use real antecedents; Cities Within Us juxtaposes ideas with reality. Antietam: A Verse Play won Honorable Mention in the 2010 War Poetry Contest by Winning Writers in Northampton, Massachusetts.

Phoenix Bunke is a song-singing, centipede-catching California child currently living in Cambridge, Massachusetts. Since graduating college, she has been up til the sky turns blue most every night, working late at a bakery and writing comics, songs and poetry.

Rachel Marsom-Richmond graduated with her M.A. from Northern Arizona University in May of 2009 and her M.F.A. from Georgia College & State University in May of 2011. Her poems have appeared in Three Line Poetry, The Bijou Poetry Review, The Camel Saloon, Quantum Poetry Magazine, and The Montucky Review. She has work forthcoming in kitchen, Camroc Press Review, Full of Crow Poetry, and The Penwood Review.

R.D. Kimball is a religious scholar, a Hawaiian shirt enthusiast, and one hell of a model American. His short stories and poems have appeared, or are forthcoming, in places like decomP, Yellow Mama, and The Red Cedar Review. He enjoys fishing, black coffee, well-stocked haberdasheries, vinyl records, and a good cigar. He lives in Portland, Oregon. Online, you can find him at http://curiousorthodoxy.wordpress.com

Richard Cody, a native Californian, has been known to write poetry and fiction. His work has appeared in many and varied print and virtual journals, and been rejected by many more! You may have seen his stories or poetry recently in Pulp Metal Magazine, Daily Love, The Carnage Conservatory, a handful of stones and Microstory a Week. He is the author of The Jewel in the Moment, Darker Corners, and This is Not My Heart – all available cheap at Lulu.com and/or Amazon.

Richard Peabody is the founder and co-editor of Gargoyle Magazine and editor (or co-editor) of nineteen anthologies including Mondo Barbie, Conversations with Gore Vidal, and A Different Beat: Writings by Women of the Beat Generation. The author of a novella, two short story collections, and six poetry books, he is also a native Washingtonian. Peabody teaches fiction writing at Johns Hopkins University, where he has been presented both the Faculty Award for Distinguished Professional Achievement (2005) and the Award for Teaching Excellence: Master of Arts in Writing

Richard Peake, a native Virginian, became a Texas resident after retiring from the University of Virginia's College at Wise. He published early poems in Impetus alongside John Ciardi and in The Georgia Review and many small journals. Collections of his poetry appeared in Wings Across... and Poems for Terence published by Vision Press, which also included poems of his in A Gathering at the Forks. He published Birds and Other Beasts in 2007. During 2008 and 2009 he won awards from Gulf Coast Poets and The Poetry Society of Texas and published in Sol Magazine and Shine Journal (one nominated for the Pushcart Prize). In 2010 he has published in Avocet, Asinine Poetry, and elsewhere.

Rick Bailey is a stay-at-home father who raised go-away kids. The poem in this issue looked ahead to this day. Alone now he divides his time between the basement and the roof and is undecided whether to go lower or higher.

Ricky Davis is pursuing an MFA in Creative Writing at Emerson College, where he studies poetry (with a special emphasis on prose poetry). His work appeared in the first issue of Prick of the Spindle in 2007. He lives in Brighton, Massachusetts with his wife and soon-to-be-born son.

Ricky Garni is a writer and designer living in North Carolina. He is presently completing a collection of tiny poems (I mean, these are teensy!) entitled WHAT'S THAT ABOUT, dutifully banged out on Faye Hunter's 1971 Smith Corona typewriter in purple cursive typeset, and dedicated with great affection to her memory.

Robert E. Petras is a graduate of West Liberty University and a resident of Toronto, Ohio. His fiction and poetry have appeared in Phantom Kangaroo Issue 13, Haunted Waters Press, Camel Saloon, Death Head Grin and Speech Bubble Magazine.

Robert McDonald's work has appeared recently in Court Green, Pank, elimae, La Petite Zine, and The Prose-Poem project, as well as issue number seven of Phantom Kangaroo. He lives in Chicago, works at an independent bookstore, and blogs at http://livesofthespiders.blogspot.com. He is almost ready to believe he is being haunted by the ghost of his sister.

Robert Vaughan's plays have been produced in N.Y.C., L.A., S.F., and Milwaukee where he resides. He leads two writing roundtables for Redbird- Redoak Studio. His prose and poetry is published in over 125 literary journals such as Elimae, BlazeVOX, and A-Minor. He is a fiction editor at JMWW magazine, and Thunderclap! Press. Also hosts Flash Fiction Fridays for WUWM's Lake Effect. His blog, One Writer's Life, is: http://rgv7735.wordpress.com.

Ron Koppelberger has been published in The Storyteller, Ceremony, Write On!!! (Poetry Magazette), Freshly Baked Fiction and Necrology Shorts.

Rose Aiello Morales is a poet currently living in Marietta, Georgia, USA. She has been writing extensively since she discovered, 10 years ago, that she was bored and had a typewriter. Since then she has appeared in various magazines and published several novels and collections of short stories and poetry. She lives with her husband Alex and an extremely spoiled cat named Moby.

Rose Arrowsmith DeCoux is a storyteller, mime and stilt-walker. She lives with her family on the shore of Lake Superior, where they run Art House B+B. Her writing has appeared in Bumples Interactive Magazine for Children, Vox Poetica, and Storytelling Magazine. For more information, visit arrowsmithdecoux.blogspot.com.

Roxanne Broda-Blake is a twenty-year-old human anatomy enthusiast, studying biological anthropology in Central New York. She likes to stitch together science and art in the leaky basement of her brain.

Roy Bentley's poems have appeared in the Southern Review, North American Review, Prairie Schooner, Shenandoah, American Literary Review, Pleiades and elsewhere. He has won a National Endowment for the Arts Creative Writing Fellowship in poetry, the Florida Division of Cultural Affairs individual artist fellowship, and six Ohio Arts Council individual artist fellowships. His latest book of poems, The Trouble with a Short Horse in Montana, won the White Pine Press poetry award in 2006. A chapbook entitled Captain America Gets Arlington Burial (Pudding House Publications: Columbus, Ohio) is due out in 2012. Lately, he makes his home in an area of Iowa often referred to as Sundown Mountain.

Ruby Darling is a Sacramento resident. She massages literary expression through Asian influences. She yodels poetry through European roots. She has no stance on stanza's, doesn't know what a soliloquy is, and has never heard of the Canterbury Tales. She's a cosmic sapling in a poetic Universe. A rare species of Euro-Asian American You.

Sarah J. Sloat is a reluctant non-smoker who works for a news agency in Germany. She has seen a flying saucer, but would be glad to be wrong. Her poems have appeared in Bateau, Court Green and Linebreak, among other publications. Her chapbook "Excuse me while I wring this long swim out of my hair" will be published by dancing girl press in 2011.

Sarah Key has had poems published in Poet Lore, Naugatuck River Review, InPatient Press, Solares Hill, Poetry Nook Magazine, Truck, Enizagam, Kaleidoscope, and the anthology My Cruel Invention. She has studied at Cave Canem with Eduardo Corral and in master workshops with Sharon Dolin and Jeanne Marie Beaumont. She has authored eight cookbooks, including a series called the Hollywood Hotplates, Serendipity Sundaes, and Serendipity Parties. Currently, she has eight essays on The Huffington Post. (http://www.huffingtonpost.com/sarah-key/) and edited the 2014 encyclopedic cookbook Gusto: The Very Best of Italian Food and Cuisine. She is privileged to work as a writing tutor at a community college in the Bronx where she learns from her students.

Scryer Veratos was born on a comet headed towards earth during the jurassic period and has been writing poetry since. He invented the lightbulb. He also has a small gnome assistant named Riri.

Seth Jani is the founder/editor of Seven CirclePress and a few other minor publications. He is obsessed with Coffee, Depth Psychology, Environmental Restoration and Rilke. His work has appeared in Writers' Bloc, The Foundling Review, Chantarelle's Notebook, Thick With Conviction and else.

Shannon Elizabeth Hardwick graduated with her Masters in Fine Arts from Sarah Lawrence College in 2010. She recently completed her first full-length manuscript of essays and poetry and has a chapbook in print. She writes in New York and Texas.

Sharon Lask Munson is the author of the chapbook, Stillness Settles Down the Lane (Uttered Chaos Press, 2010) and a full-length book of poems, That Certain Blue (Blue Light Press, 2011). She publishes widely in literary journals and anthologies. She lives in Eugene, Oregon.

Sheila Hassell Hughes is Associate Professor and Chair of English, and former Director of Women's and Gender Studies, at the University of Dayton. She earned her BA (British Columbia) and MA (Toronto) in English and her PhD (Emory) in women's studies. Her research foci include gender and religion in American Indian women's writing and the voices of girls in urban schools, and her poetry explores modes of loss, recovery, and connection. She has published scholarly articles and poems in journals such as MELUS: Multi-Ethnic Literatures of the U.S., SAIL: Studies in American Indian Literatures, African American Review, American Quarterly, Religion and Literature, Literature and Theology, Mused, and the Lullwater Review.

Simon Jacobs continues to attend an aggravatingly tiny college in the Middle West. He has contributed to Thought Catalog, and his fiction has appeared in Monkeybicycle and is forthcoming in Do Hookers Kiss? His blog of artistic pursuits resides at emoboysandgirls.tumblr.com.

Simon Perchik is an attorney whose poems have appeared in Partisan Review, The Nation, Poetry, The New Yorker, and elsewhere. His most recent collection is Almost Rain, published by River Otter Press (2013). For more information, including free e-books, his essay titled "Magic, Illusion and Other Realities" please visit his website at www.simonperchik.com.

Stephen Bunch lives and writes in Lawrence, Kansas, where he received the 2008 Langston Hughes Award for Poetry from the Lawrence Arts Center and Raven Books.

His poems can be found in Autumn Sky Poetry, The Externalist, The Literary Bohemian, Phantom Kangaroo, Fickle Muses, IthacaLit, and Umbrella. From 1978 to 1988, he edited and published Tellus, a little magazine that featured work by Victor Contoski, Edward Dorn, Jane Hirshfield, Donald Levering, Denise Low, Paul Metcalf, Edward Sanders, and many others. After a fifteen-year hibernation, he awoke in 2005 and resumed writing. Preparing to Leave, his first gathering of poems, was published in 2011. His collection DisquiEtudes recently appeared in Mudlark. Bunch can be found on the Map of Kansas Literature near L. Frank Baum and Gwendolyn Brooks. [He reports that property values tanked when he moved into the neighborhood.

Steve Castro's poems have appeared in Grey Sparrow Journal, Everyday Genius, Underground Voices, Splash of Red, ASKEW, Chiricú, Snow Jewel - a Grey Sparrow Press publication, Divine Dirt Quarterly, Andar21 (Galiza / Galicia, Spain) and they are forthcoming in Cricket Online Review and The Caterpillar Chronicles. His flash fiction can be found in This Great Society. Birthplace: San José, Costa Rica.

Steve Isaak, sometimes published as Nikki Isaak and Chuck Lovepoe, is the author of several poetry anthologies. He is the editor of Reading & Writing By Pub Light, www. readingbypublight.blogspot.com.

Steve Toase is a writer and archaeologist who lives in North Yorkshire, England and occasionally Munich, Germany. For the past eighteen months he has been sending out little ghosts disguised as stories to haunt various online magazines such as Cafe Irreal, Street Cake Magazine, nthposition and Byker Books. So far twelve have found new homes in the wider world. When not writing Steve spends his time trying to keep old British motorbikes on the road. Occasionally he succeeds. To read more of Steve's work please visit www.stevetoase.co.uk.

Susie Swanton's poetry has appeared in the cream city review, MUZZLE Magazine, and decomP magazinE. She performed in the entry of The Encyclopedia Show in Chicago that featured slices of John Wayne Gacy's brain.

Tamer Mostafa is a Stockton, California resident who recently completed his degree in Creative Writing from UC Davis.

Tammy Ho Lai-Ming is a Hong Kong-born writer currently based in London, UK. She is a founding co-editor of Cha: An Asian Literary Journal. More at www.sighming. com.

Tannen Dell is a writer from Tigard, Oregon. He edits at Indigo Rising Magazine and PCC's Alchemy/Alembic; two fine publications with alot of new age and up-in-coming material in them.

Tanuj Solanki works in an insurance firm in Bombay. He is 24. His work has been published in elimae; Short, Fast and Deadly;Boston Literary Magazine; Yes, Poetry, and others. He is currently completing a short story collection about fatalism in Indian cities, titled The Bom Bay of Life. He just can't learn swimming.

Taylor Graham is a volunteer search-and-rescue dog handler in the Sierra Nevada. She's included in the anthologies Villanelles (Everyman's Library) and California Poetry: From the Gold Rush to the Present (Santa Clara University). Her book The Downstairs Dance Floor was awarded the Robert Phillips Poetry Chapbook Prize. Her latest book is What the Wind Says (Lummox Press, 2013), poems about living and working with her canine search partners over the past 40 years.

Tess Joyce has recently squeezed a poem into the December issue of Anatomy and Etymology. In 2009 a collection of her poetry was published in Delhi, India; the book was a collaboration with an Indian writer. She lives with her partner in Indonesia and in 2011 was the Communications Officer for Dr Galdikas, to write out about her orangutan rehabilitation centre.

Tess Pfeifle is eighteen years old, likes camping, abandoned insane asylums and unsolved mysteries.

Theodosia Henney has just returned from several months of travel, and is intensely grateful to be back at her laptop, deleting piles of spam for porn, bamboo flooring, and LDS singles. Her work has appeared or is forthcoming in over a dozen publications, including Ghost Ocean Magazine, Blossombones, Grey Sparrow Press, and Fifth Wednesday Journal.

Thomas Piekarski appeared in Agni, New York Quarterly, Paris Review, Southern Review, Ploughshares, and others. His first book was published in 2010 by Nimbus Press.

Tony Walton is a Caribbean writer living in the Cayman Islands. His works have appeared in Storyteller Magazine, Moonkind Press, Whisperings Magazine, Mountain Tales Press, Out of Our Magazine, Poetry Bay Magazine, Burningword Magazine, Wilde Magazine, Nite Writers Literary International Literary Journal, Avalon Literary Review, Iceland Daily, East Lit Literary Magazine, Boston Poetry Magazine, Eunoia Magazine, Olentangy Review, Carnival Literary Magazine and Verity LA.

Tyler Burdwood plays music in a band called bellwire and likes to write poetry. He attends Lesley University in Cambridge, Massachusetts.

Ty Russell is a recent graduate of the University of Pennsylvania. His work has been published in Apiary Magazine, The Pennsylvania Gazette, Peregrine, at RelevantMagazine.com, and earned an honorable mention in Glimmer Train's 2009 Short Story Contest and Stony Brook's 2010 Short Fiction Contest. He lives in north central Pennsylvania with his wife and their children.

Vanessa Young is the executive director of a nonprofit arts organization in New Jersey and a graduate of Fordham University in New York City.

Veronica McDonald lives in San Diego with her husband, two toddlers, and two black cats. She received her MA in Literature from American University. Her short fiction can be found in Beorh Weekly and Scrutiny. Check her out on her website.

Vivian Bird loves palm trees and Old Hollywood. She writes everyday.

Walter Bjorkman is a writer, poet and photographer from Brooklyn, NY now residing in the mountains of Pennsylvania. His poems and short stories have appeared in various issues of Poets & Artists, O&S, Wilderness House Literary Review, Blue Print Review, Metazen, Dark Chaos, OCHO and MiPoesias. His collection of short stories, Elsie's World, was published in January 2011. He is Associate Editor of THRUSH Poetry Journal.

Walter Conley got his start writing comic books. His poetry and fiction appear in the small press, anthologies and at such websites as Danse Macabre, Gloom Cupboard and In Between Altered States. He draws banner art for A Twist of Noir and a monthly comic for Pulp Metal Magazine. His current project, as editor, is the e-book series Flashdrive. Walter lives in VA and his blog, Back Again and Gone, is at http://baag2009.blogspot.com.

Walt Garner has been teaching in a public school for sixteen years, and though he hasn't had a motorcycle gang after him yet, he's had a large number of weirdos gunning for him – if only in his dreams.

Wayne F. Burke's poetry has appeared in Bluestem, the bicycle review, Red Savina, Forge, Insert, Black Wire, Curbside Splendor, The commonline Journal, and elsewhere. His book of poems WORDS THAT BURN is published by Bareback Press (2013).

Wendy Willis is a poet, mother, and democracy builder who lives and works in Portland, Oregon. Her peripatetic lifestyle that allows her to make dinner in Portland one night and be at work in the coalfields of West Virginia the next lends to her poems a lexicon of the Republic with a strong dash of the domestic. She is the interim director of the Policy Consensus Initiative and has published poems in a variety of regional and national journals including VoiceCatcher, the Bellingham Review and Poetry Northwest. Wendy lives in Southeast Portland with her two daughters, her husband and his son, and their two unruly dogs.

Wesley Dylan Gray resides in Florida with his wife, Brenda and daughter, Elizabeth Jadzia. In his spare time, he writes; with these words he attempts to exude a disposition of resplendent contrast, writing things of light and of darkness, things of beauty and of the grotesque. Such writings can be found in various small press magazines and anthologies. Find him online at www.wesleydylangray.com.

William C. Blome is a writer of poetry and short fiction. He beds down nightly in-between Baltimore and Washington, DC, and he is an MA graduate of the Johns Hopkins University Writing Seminars. His work has previously seen the light of day in such fine little mags as Amarillo Bay, Prism International, Taj Mahal Review, Pure Francis, This, Salted Feathers and The California Quarterly.

William Doreski's work has appeared in various e and print journals and in several collections, most recently Waiting for the Angel (Pygmy Forest Press, 2009).

William Page's poems have appeared widely in such print and e journals as THE NORTH AMERICAN REVIEW, SOUTHWEST REVIEW, THE SEWANEE REVIEW, RATTLE, and THE PEDESTAL. He is founding editor of THE PINCH and has published four collections of poems including the award winning BODIES NOT OUR OWN and WILLIAM PAGE GREATEST HITS 1970-2000 from Pudding House Publications in Ohio.

Willie Smith is deeply ashamed of being human. His work celebrates this horror.

INDEX